The Rowman & Littlefield Guide to Learning Center Administration

THEORY & PRACTICE FOR PEER TUTORS AND LEARNING CENTER PROFESSIONALS

Series Advisors:
Daniel R. Sanford, Bates College
Michelle Steiner, Marymount University

The series *Theory & Practice for Peer Tutors and Learning Center Professionals* serves the international scholarly and professional communities associated with peer tutoring in higher education. With contributions that address the multiple audiences of learning center professionals, scholars of peer-led learning, and peer educators, the series aims to advance the scholarship and practice of peer-led learning by enriching it with contributions from the broader scholarship of teaching and learning, and by building connections across the many areas of praxis that share the uniquely effective and impactful pedagogy of peer tutoring.

Titles in Series:

The Rowman & Littlefield Guide for Peer Tutors by Daniel R. Sanford
The Rowman & Littlefield Guide to Learning Center Administration by Daniel R. Sanford and Michelle Steiner

The Rowman & Littlefield Guide to Learning Center Administration

Leading Peer Tutoring Programs in Higher Education

Daniel R. Sanford and Michelle Steiner

ROWMAN & LITTLEFIELD
Lanham • Boulder • New York • London

Published by Rowman & Littlefield
An imprint of The Rowman & Littlefield Publishing Group, Inc.
4501 Forbes Boulevard, Suite 200, Lanham, Maryland 20706
www.rowman.com

6 Tinworth Street, London, SE11 5AL, United Kingdom

British Library Cataloguing in Publication Information Available

Library of Congress Cataloging-in-Publication Data
Names: Sanford, Daniel R., 1980–, author. | Steiner, Michelle, author.
Title: The Rowman & Littlefield guide to administering learning and peer tutoring
    centers / Daniel R. Sanford and Michelle Steiner.
Description: Lanham : The Rowman & Littlefield Publishing Group, 2021. | Series:
    Theory & practice for peer tutors and learning center professionals | Includes
    bibliographical references and index. | Summary: "The only comprehensive, practical
    resource for successfully establishing and administering a campus learning center"—
    Provided by publisher.
Identifiers: LCCN 2020056603 (print) | LCCN 2020056604 (ebook) | ISBN
    9781538154618 (cloth) | ISBN 9781538154625 (paperback) | ISBN 9781538154632
    (ebook)
Subjects: LCSH: Classroom learning centers—Administration. | Laboratory schools—
    Administration.
Classification: LCC LB3044.8 .S36 2021 (print) | LCC LB3044.8 (ebook) | DDC
    378.1/797—dc23
LC record available at https://lccn.loc.gov/2020056603
LC ebook record available at https://lccn.loc.gov/2020056604

∞™ The paper used in this publication meets the minimum requirements of
American National Standard for Information Sciences—Permanence of Paper
for Printed Library Materials, ANSI/NISO Z39.48-1992.

Contents

Preface

Learning centers are as varied as the institutions where they occur and the student bodies they serve. They can be extremely large, occupying a dedicated space with a significant professional staff and ample budget. They can be exceedingly small, managed by a single coordinator who oversees a handful of tutors in a single room. They can support the entire academic curriculum or focus on one aspect of it (writing, mathematics, language learning). They can serve the entire student body or one segment of it (engineering students, graduate students, students of color). They can grow out of or draw on a number of different traditions of academic support, including content tutoring, writing tutoring, supplemental instruction, TRIO, quantitative literacy programs, academic coaching, and other models. What learning centers all have in common, and what makes a learning center a learning center, however, is peer tutoring. Within a learning center, students—selected based on their academic and personal qualifications and trained in the pedagogy of peer-led learning—work to support their fellow students as learners. Learning centers leverage successful students to ensure that every student has the support to succeed and excel.

This book is for learning center administrators. Whether you're a learning center director or a manager/coordinator of a program within a larger center, the goal of this text is to provide you with everything you need to accomplish your goals (except a space and budget, of course, for which you're on your own—although we hope to offer some helpful guidance), drawing on a well-established set of best practices that have emerged out of the professional community of higher education learning centers, as well as from our own hard-won experience as learning center directors.

This is a nuts-and-bolts book. You can expect everything you need to know about administering a learning center and nothing you don't. This book is the companion text to *The Rowman & Littlefield Guide for Peer Tutors* (Sanford, 2020); the two books together form a complete introduction to the theory and practice of peer tutoring. The *Guide for Peer Tutors* provides more information on the theory that underlies learning centers and peer tutoring, as well as a more in-depth treatment of key topics such as tutoring across diversity, online pedagogies, strategies for learning, and the affective aspects of peer tutoring. Forthcoming volumes in the series will provide more in-depth inquiry—including the state of the field, extant variation in best practices, and unanswered research questions—into many of the same topics covered here. The goal of this book is to provide professionals new to the field with an introduction and port of entry to the field and experienced professionals with a way to compare their own center to an established set of best practices. Each chapter outlines one aspect of learning center administration, closing with a checklist that can be used as a rubric for self-evaluation, goal-setting, and planning.

It is a remarkably common experience for people in our field to be dropped, without significant training or experience, into the task of organizing a tutoring program. If this is you, know that you are not alone. Many others like you are out there, and you are part of a highly supportive, welcoming national community of learning center professionals. Know, also, that the skills, background, and training that you bring to the field are relevant and will inform your unique approach to learning center administration. Speaking, if we may, on behalf of the field, we're glad to have you.

One final note: variation is good. Excellent centers have arrived at solutions to the problems learning centers commonly face that are different from the approaches we've outlined here. Our hope is to give you a template that reflects a standard model. Depart from it as you will, with intention and planning. Be sure to present a case study to let all of us know how it went!

Acknowledgments

Thank you to all of my current and former colleagues at the Center for Academic Program Support at the University of New Mexico, and at the Academic Resource Commons at Bates College—mistakes are the best teacher, and you've seen me learn a lot! Thank you to my coauthor, friend, and mentor, Michelle, who I'm so pleased to find myself working closely with once again. Thank you to our editor, Mark Kerr, for his feedback and vision on this book and the series of which it is a part. And thank you to my family for your patience and support.

—Daniel

Thank you to colleagues, past and present, from the University of Minnesota, University of New Mexico, George Washington University, and Marymount University. Everyone I've worked with has provided me with insight and unique perspectives on supporting students—I'm better at what I do because of you. Thank you to my most trusted mentor, Karen Olson—you are the reason that I am confident in leading student success centers and initiatives with grace and skill. To my coauthor and one of my favorite people on the planet, Daniel Sanford: I am a better thinker and learner because of our relationship; I appreciate you challenging me to work on this series with you. Thank you, Mark Kerr—your enthusiasm for this project propelled us forward! Finally, to Jon and Xavier—I dedicate this book to you both; your positivity surrounding this endeavor has led to a miraculous final product—I love you very much.

—Michelle

From both of us, from the bottom of our hearts: thank you to the profoundly supportive, welcoming community of academic support professionals, and in particular to all of you who are so giving of your time and energy on the LRNASST and WCENTER lists. We've received unbelievable benefit from all of you heroes who take the time to share your knowledge and expertise in these forums, and we hope that this book can repay some of that benefit in kind to new individuals entering the field.

Chapter One

Learning Centers in Higher Education

Learning centers play a unique role on college and university campuses. On the one hand, they are intimately connected with every aspect of the curriculum, perhaps more wholly a part of the institution than any other single program within a college or university. Learning centers intersect with courses and programs of study from across the full spectrum of academic disciplines that comprise the academy. The competencies over which learning centers engage learners (writing, quantitative reasoning, problem solving, study skills, metacognitive strategies) cut across every aspect of the curriculum, affecting students' success not only in specific courses or programs but in their studies overall. Learning centers interact with students at multiple levels (from introductory to advanced) and in many ways (as clients, as employees, and as stakeholders). Learning centers exist at the center. They're a hub that connects many aspects of the academy and many aspects of the student experience, providing a space (whether physical or virtual) for students to connect over the shared challenges of being a student.

Conceived in another way, however, learning centers stand apart. Although most aspects of higher education are organized around implementing curricula, holding students (regardless of background, disposition, or previous education experiences) to the objective standards of a course of study, learning centers are organized around engaging with students as unique learners. Although many other forms of institutional academic support are offered on the model of remediation, "extra" help that students need before they can fully engage with the content of standard courses, learning centers interweave support throughout the curriculum, ensuring that every student has the tools to succeed. And whereas most venues for higher education are defined by the culture of classroom learning, with norms and standards determined by faculty and professional staff, learning centers are defined by the culture of students, and by the norms and standards of successful learners.

THE LEARNING CENTER AS A
MODEL FOR ACADEMIC SUPPORT

Tremendous variation exists within higher education learning centers. Individual centers may occupy a large dedicated space or operate wholly out of borrowed spaces. They may occupy brick and mortar buildings, online spaces, or some combination of the two. Administratively, a learning center may comprise a single administrative unit under the leadership of a director, or it may represent the collaborative efforts of multiple units that deliver different aspects of academic support but present themselves as a unified suite of programming (often through a shared physical space, functioning as a learning commons where students can access comprehensive support). A broad spectrum of programming types is encompassed within learning centers, which in many centers includes not only services that students provide, but also those implemented by a professional staff or faculty: academic coaching, for example, or courses on general skills for academic success.

And while centers operating under the name of "learning centers" generally engage with all students across the entire curriculum, a variety of programs that focus on a single area/aspect of the curriculum (e.g., writing, mathematics, language learning) or on a specific segment of the student population (e.g., engineering students, graduate students, first-gen students) can be construed as types of learning centers, specializing in ways that are highlighted to students by program names and identities and have their own unique histories, traditions, and areas of scholarship. The learning center model comfortably accommodates such a large degree of variation precisely because the core identity of learning centers is so strong. Although individual centers may vary from the prototypical learning center in any of the ways described here and countless others, they have a strong core of shared history, theoretical underpinnings, and best practices that powerfully unite and define higher education learning centers across all of their many and varied instantiations.

Learning centers are driven by active and collaborative approaches to learning. One of the most consistent and powerful research outcomes from the past five decades of education and psychology research is the finding that learning is far more effective and thorough at all levels—from basic retention of information, to deeper forms of learning associated with higher educational outcomes—when learners actively engage with ideas and concepts (Bonwell & Eison, 1991; Chickering & Gamson, 1987; Crouch & Mazur, 2001; Fagen,

A BRIEF HISTORY OF HIGHER EDUCATION LEARNING CENTERS

Higher education learning centers and writing centers, in their current form with an emphasis on peer-led learning, emerged (along with other models for peer-led learning, such as supplemental instruction) in the same historical moment in the 1970s (Arendale, 2004; Boquet, 1999; Bruffee, 1984). During this time, the national conception of higher education was undergoing a significant shift. Challenged by the open admissions movement (which advocated for greatly lowering admissions criteria in order to reduce discrimination and fulfill the responsibility of colleges and universities to serve all segments of society) to facilitate broader access to higher education, many colleges and universities found themselves grappling with the challenge of a student body instantiating a far more diverse array of preparatory experiences than had been the case for previous generations of students.

The nascent learning centers (generally going by the terms "learning resource center" or "learning assistance center") that emerged in this era (Christ, 1971; Devirian, Enright, & Smith, 1975; Hultgren, 1970; Peterson, 1975; Tillerson, 1973; Walker et al., 1974) distinguished themselves from previous forms of academic support in two main ways: first, whereas tutorial services had previously been targeted toward specific groups of students who were seen as underprepared, at-risk, or not performing at a predetermined level, learning centers were for all students. By focusing on the shared challenges that all learners face rather than on the specific needs of targeted groups, learning centers sought to erase the stigma associated with academic support, profiling it as a part of every student's experience rather than as the purview of groups targeted for "extra help."

The second was peer tutoring. Learning centers (along with writing centers and SI programs) effected a complete shift in the culture of academic support by focusing on students as educators. Previous iterations of academic support (with a few isolated historical exceptions) were generally implemented by faculty or other professionals, and therefore operated as extensions of classrooms and the culture thereof. Learning centers and writing centers established an alternate space, with a culture determined by students rather than by faculty. The role of professionals became to train and facilitate students to support one another, learning centers serving as venues for collaborative learning in which students work together in mutually beneficial learning interactions. Learning centers, alongside other forms of peer support, have changed and grown as new currents have shaped higher education, as the field has moved beyond developmental education toward an emphasis on the relevance of learning centers to all students, and as learning center theory has been enriched with the vast scholarship of teaching and learning that has emerged since the widespread implementation of peer tutoring as a model for academic support. These concepts—relevance to all students, peer-led learning, and collaborative learning—have continued to be the core around which the identity of learning centers concentrates.

Crouch, & Mazur, 2002; Freeman et al., 2014; Haak et al., 2011; Hake, 1998; Knight & Wood, 2005; Smith et al., 2009). When learners use information to solve problems, accomplish tasks, and craft arguments, they integrate it within their structures for knowledge: everything they already know and their view of the world. Through this process, not only is information retained more effectively (such that it can later be recalled in assessments and serve as a basis for further learning in subsequent courses), but it is also effectively contextualized, placed in a meaningful relationship to everything else that a learner knows (or is learning) about a topic. *All* learning is active learning—nothing is learned if it's not integrated with existing knowledge structures.

Nonetheless, more passive forms of learning, in which learners are the recipients of information presented to them by instructors, remain the default mode of instruction in higher education. This is not to say that it's not possible for students to learn in environments that place them in a passive role (they can, by adopting a critical and inquisitive mental stance toward the information being presented to them), nor that active learning is never found in classroom environments (the efforts of our colleagues in faculty development programs such as centers for teaching and writing across the curriculum, have served to make such active approaches far more common in higher education). In learning centers, however, active approaches are the norm. A core tenet of learning center theory is to ensure that students are active, engaged participants within their own processes for learning, and students who use the services of learning centers are supported in assuming agency in their own processes for learning.

In collaborative approaches to learning, students engage in tasks and processes in peer groups rather than individually, often through structured learning interactions. One reason for the effectiveness of collaborative approaches to learning (Capar & Tarim, 2015; Miller & Santana-Vega, 2006; Puzio & Colby, 2013; Slavin, 1992; Springer, Stanne, & Donovan, 1999) is that collaborative learning is a powerful form of active learning: when learners approach tasks in groups, they are forced to engage in the active processes of evaluating others' ideas and arguments and articulating their own ideas in ways that will persuade others.

Just as powerfully, in collaborative learning environments two effects take place: less advanced students have modeled for them the way in which more advanced learners approach the relevant task, and the way to internalize it and incorporate it within their own method. More advanced learners can articulate their own skills and knowledge in ways that will be accessible to students at a lower level of mastery, which reinforces and clarifies their own thinking. Finally, in collaborative learning environments students are exposed to multiple approaches to an idea, problem, or concept. Each individual within a group contributes to a more complex, layered understanding of an idea that emerges within the group (and can, in turn, be internalized by each individual). Learning centers are focused on bringing students together in collaborative learning environments that function as communities for learning (Gabelnick et al., 1990; Laufgraben & Shapiro, 2004; Lenning & Ebbers, 1999; Shapiro & Levine, 1999; Smith et al., 2004; Tinto, Russo, & Kadel, 1994) in which students at all levels of ability, and representing diverse points of view, work toward shared educational outcomes in ways that are mutually enriching.

Learning centers are student-led, student-serving spaces. Deciding who should and should not be at the institution, holding students to objective criteria, enforcing academic standards, serving as gatekeepers to courses and curricula: more than enough programming is in place, at every institution, to accomplish these goals. Learning centers exist to support learners, meeting all students, without judgment, wherever they are in their journey as learners. They provide support for learners in their continuous growth and development toward mastery of the information, ideas, and skills that are explicit within academic curricula; and the strategies, approaches, and mind-sets that are implicit within them. They help learners to accomplish their academic goals, whatever those goals may be and wherever students may be in their paths toward attaining them.

Learning centers support diverse learners. Modern institutions of higher education, even when taking to heart most seriously an inclusive and equitable mission, are the inheritors of a model of education that is highly Eurocentric and traditionally exclusionary toward members of society not falling within a narrow, highly discriminatory conception of what a college student looks like (white, male, nondisabled) and who colleges and universities exist to serve (the wealthy elite). Even as higher education has come to be reconceptualized more broadly, the tendency persists to treat white, cisgendered, nondisabled, middle- to upper-class students as the default audience for instruction. Higher education tends to privilege native speakers of whatever variety is most valued within society, coding as "correct" those forms of language that align most directly with wealth and power. Colleges and universities also have a tendency to reward those learners who perform well in certain formats of instruction (reading and lecture) and in certain modes of assessment (writing academic essays, taking exams) while failing to provide alternate modes of learning and assessment for learners who may learn and demonstrate their mastery of course content more effectively in other ways. Learning centers seek to make the institutions that they occur within as accessible as possible for every learner by fully welcoming a diverse student body and providing support for every learner across differences in race, language, culture, gender identity, sexual orientation, physical ability, and neurodivergence.

Learning centers are spaces for students to do (and in doing, learn how to do) the work of being a student—studying for exams, doing homework, reviewing their notes, completing course readings, writing papers—in a supported environment where help is easily accessible in the immediate environment. Pursuing a college degree can be an isolating experience. Learning centers offer a space for fellowship and community with other students who are facing similar challenges, who can serve as a support network and as collaborators in the enterprise of learning. Learning is *possible* in any venue, and often the college students who excel are those who are able to bring an active mind-set to educational environments that tend to place students in a passive role. Learning centers are spaces *optimized* for learning. By making active and collaborative approaches the default pedagogies of the space, and by in all ways (by the visual and auditory physical environment, through the emotional tone set by employees, by means of easy access to educational resources, and in as many other ways as possible) placing the needs of students at the fore, learning centers create an environment as conducive to learning as possible, for as many variations of learners as possible. Within the learning environment the center creates, every student has the opportunity to develop academic habits, understand course concepts, and experiment with strategies for solving disciplinary problems in ways that can then be transferred into other, higher-stakes educational environments.

The support that learning centers provide for learners may take a number of different forms, including those that a professional staff of faculty implement. The central, defining attribute of learning centers, however—the core pedagogy that defines our field, and the fundamental organizing principle underlying every aspect of learning center administration—is peer tutoring.

PEER TUTORING

Peer tutoring is a model in which students provide academic support for other students. Tutors, within a peer support model, aren't intended to be experts but, rather, slightly more advanced (relative to the students they are working with) learners. In many formats of education, the primary role of the educator is to serve as an authority in the field or discipline. In peer tutoring, the primary role of the educator is to serve as a guide, resource, and mentor, creating the conditions for effective learning and providing support for learners to make continuous progress toward their academic goals. We can think of a student's progress through the courses in a curriculum as a continuous journey toward mastery: the point at which an individual is able to fluently and capably use the terminology, ideas, conventions, frameworks, and strategies of an academic discipline to operate independently and confidently within a field of professional practice, to arrive at new insights that make a meaningful contribution to a domain of inquiry, or to attain other thresholds defined within particular fields of professional and academic practice. Faculty and instructors represent individuals who, while they continue to grow as learners, have completed the journey toward mastery that students are undertaking. Peer tutors, on the other hand, are fellow travelers. As students who were recently at the same point in their journey as learners that students using the center are now, they are able to offer empathy, guidance, support, and mentorship based on their own recent experience.

Students continually encounter, as they progress through a curriculum, new ideas, new challenges, and new types of information. The center is a space where students operate at the limits of their abilities, building on their current knowledge to solve new kinds of problems and accomplish new kinds of tasks. Peer tutors engage with learners, ask questions, and build relationships that help them to ascertain where learners are in their journey toward mastery and what issues may be preventing them from progressing. Peer tutors then provide support—hints, questions, examples, alternate explanations, and other interventions—for learners to be able to accomplish tasks that would otherwise be beyond their abilities, allowing them to reap the learning benefits of accomplishing them in much the same way weightlifters achieve a strength-building benefit from lifting an amount of weight that they are only capable of safely attempting with the help of a spotter. Through the support (known as *scaffolding*) that more advanced learners provide, learners are able to develop more complex structures of knowledge and grow in mastery. Concepts and problems that students once needed the support of a tutor to engage with become tasks that they are able to accomplish independently, and students are able to transfer educational gains made within the supported learning environment of the center to other, higher-stakes educational venues. Peer tutoring is constructivist, in that the focus of peer tutoring interactions isn't to relay knowledge from one individual to another but, rather, to support learners in building knowledge for themselves.

Within the collaborative learning environment of the learning center, students have the benefit of seeing how other learners engage with the same types of problems and tasks with which they are currently grappling. In the process, they are able to adopt successful strategies that more advanced learners use. In many cases, this is a role that peer tutors fill. They serve as attainable models for the students they engage with in learning interactions, demonstrating the problem-solving skills, academic habits, and strategies for learning that will empower learners to succeed within an academic curriculum. In other cases, peer tutors may serve as facilitators of interactions between groups of peers, creating groups within which students at different levels of mastery and ability collaborate toward a common goal. In the process, less advanced students have the benefit of modeling from their more advanced peers, while more advanced students benefit from the active learning task of articulating their understanding of course concepts in a way that is accessible to students less versed in them. All of the students within such a group accrue the collaborative learning benefit of engaging with learners who may have points of view different from their own and negotiating varying ideas of correctness. In all of these roles, peer tutors support students in their growth as independent learners by empowering them to leverage more advanced learners to propel their own progress toward mastery.

PEER TUTORING AS A HIGH-IMPACT PRACTICE

Higher education theorist George Kuh, based on results from the National Survey of Student Engagement (a massive research project, spanning hundreds of institutions, to map student engagement and student learning outcomes against organizational behaviors and educational practices), identified the attributes of practices that have a clear, demonstrable effect on student engagement and student achievement (Kuh, 2015; Kuh, Schneider, & Association of American Colleges and Universities, 2008; Whitt, Schuh, Kinzie, & Kuh, 2013). These high-impact educational practices (or HIPs) require students to devote large amounts of time and effort to purposeful tasks, interact intensively with faculty and peers, engage with people different from themselves, operate in new settings, and engage in active, collaborative learning. HIPs have received a large amount of attention in higher education, because they have a well-documented effect on student retention and student success, having the highest impact on the least prepared students, students with low test scores, and students from historically underserved populations.

Peer tutoring is a HIP par excellence, on several levels. First, it's impactful for the students who use it. In learning centers, students explore connections across courses and the relevance of course material to their own experience. They spend time on task in a scaffolded learning environment, practicing and applying skills learned in class. They engage in collaborative learning activities that challenge them to work with other students. They form connections with their peers. They apply active learning strategies to course material. For all of these reasons, peer tutoring works, which we see clearly documented in a wide range of studies indicating the effectiveness of peer tutoring as a form of academic intervention (e.g., Arco-Tirado, Fernández-Martín & Fernández-Balboa, 2011; Colver & Fry, 2016; Comfort & McMahon, 2014; Cooper, 2010; Grillo & Leist, 2014; Hendriksen et al., 2005; Kostecki & Bers, 2008; Munley, Garvey, & McConnell, 2010; Reinheimer et al., 2010; Xu, Hartman, Uribe, & Mencke, 2014; Zha, Estes, & Xu, 2019).

Second, peer tutoring is a HIP for peer tutors. Tutors, through their work in learning centers, continually explore connections between lower- and higher-division coursework. They develop a deeper understanding of course content through ongoing engagement. They invest in the curriculum. They explore applying knowledge in different venues. They assume a leadership role in the university. And they make connections between their identity as a student and their identity as a professional that they will carry into their lives beyond the academy. One way in which we see these results is a clear academic benefit from tutoring for tutors (Arco-Tirado, Fernández-Martín, & Fernández-Balboa, 2011; Beasley, 1997; Colvin, 2007; Galbraith & Winterbottom, 2011; Jones & Kolko, 2005; Keenan, 2014).

Finally, peer tutoring unlocks the potential of other educational venues to function as HIPs. In learning centers, students combine academic achievement with social engagement, and they work in concert with the curriculum and other support services to provide a more engaging student experience. Learning centers make institutions more effective in their educational mission, by enriching academic curricula with a space devoted to supported engagement in purposeful tasks, intense interaction across peer groups, the transfer of course content to new educational venues, and active, collaborative learning.

THE ROLE OF LEARNING CENTER ADMINISTRATORS

Learning centers are complex and varied, encompassing many spheres of learning and many different types of programming. Learning centers are always, however—above all else, and at the heart of our identity as a field—sites for peer tutoring. The work that peer tutors accomplish *is* the work of the center. As learning administrators—or LCAs—our primary role is always to guide, support, and facilitate that work. We accomplish this by

- leading, setting a clear vision of our centers for our tutors and other groups of stakeholders;
- creating environments that are optimized for learning and collaborative interaction that lead to a productive, mutually enriching exchange of knowledge, skills, and aptitudes between students at different levels of educational advancement;
- ensuring that tutors have access, through tutor training, to principles and pedagogies (gleaned from relevant fields of educational research) to guide their interactions with learners, by creating a shared vision that guides the collaborative efforts of teams of peer tutors who work alongside others to support learners, and by creating a culture of learning and active engagement; and

- ensuring as broad and widespread access as possible to the benefits of peer tutoring, for both tutors and learners, at our institutions.

On our campuses, we work to create and maintain healthy relationships with students, faculty, administrators, and staff stakeholders to ensure productive collaborations and to cultivate widespread awareness of the services that our centers provide. We continually gather, analyze, and distribute data on usage of our services and the effect of our services on student success to create general cognizance within the institutions that our centers serve of the effectiveness of peer tutoring in increasing student success and supporting the missions of the colleges and universities within which our programs are embedded. We seek, through all of the channels at our disposal (institutional leadership, grants, donors, campus partnerships), adequate space and funding for our centers to accomplish the outcomes that we've articulated for them, to fully meet student needs, and to grow and develop to meet new challenges. We navigate tensions between what a learning center is (a site for peer-led learning, a central part of the student experience for every learner, a vital hub for collaborations centered around active and collaborative learning), and how others might misperceive or erroneously envision it (a site for remediation, a peripheral program relevant to only a small subset of underperforming students, a center for reinforcing curricular norms and standards). We strive continually to guarantee that everyone is aware of the center, the services that it provides, and the ways that it's available to support the student success efforts of others on campus. That includes students who would benefit from the services the center provides; faculty and advisors who provide referrals to peer tutoring; units with whom we could potentially collaborate in strategic efforts to provide support for specific groups of students, instructors, or entire departments that could benefit from the expertise fostered within the center on peer-led learning and student leadership.

We advocate for students. Learning centers don't exist to support faculty, they don't exist to support academic departments, they don't exist to serve students' parents, and they don't exist to support administrative priorities. As much as our goals may frequently align, and as much as partners at each of these levels can serve as powerful allies in our work, our ultimate goal is not to bolster the efforts of any of these groups. Learning centers exist to serve students, and as learning center administrators, our voice on campus is the voice of an advocate for students. We advocate for support and recognition for the work that students accomplish as tutors and for the right of every student to receive the support to succeed and excel in higher education. When our goals depart from others on campus—over issues of students' control of information about their use of the center, over whether students belong on campus or in a specific program—we are on the side of students.

These are ideals, and in practice none of them may ever be fully accomplished. Many of the long-term strategic goals that we may hold for ourselves and for our centers (or for programs within them) are the work of a career, not an academic term. And perhaps the most universal defining trait of an LCA is that we are working with realities on the ground: few of us would claim to have fully adequate space or funding to fully accomplish our mission, and making the most of the resources at your disposal is an essential skill. You're working with the realities on your campus. As you do, the shared values that define our field are touchstones in advancing the goals of your program and supporting the essential work of peer tutoring.

QUESTIONS FOR PROGRAM ASSESSMENT

- Does the center support the historical mission of learning centers to ensure broad access to higher education?
- Does the center focus on active approaches to learning that provide students with an alternative to the more passive learning environments commonly found in classrooms and actively mentor students to assume a role of active agency in their own processes for learning?
- Does the center focus on collaborative approaches to learning that place learners together in venues where students can come in contact with diverse points of view and in which less advanced learners can observe and emulate the strategies that more advanced learners use to solve problems and approach their studies?
- Does the center make peer-led learning a central pedagogy, placing students in the role of academic mentors who provide scaffolding for their fellow students as they engage in the work of being a student?
- Does the center position service to students at the center of its mission and identity, advocating for students and making strategic decisions based on the interests of the students it serves?
- Does the leadership of the center have a clear vision for the role that students play in the center?
- Does the leadership of the center have a clear vision for the center's role in advocating for student learners?
- Does the leadership of the center have a clear vision of the difference between how other departments and programs at your institution approach student learning and how your center approaches student learning?

Chapter Two

Program Structure, Vision, and Mission

Every institution has its own highly complex story of how it emerged at its current landscape of academic support. We are, as learning center administrators on our home campuses, the inheritors of patchwork quilts of programming that have emerged within our institutions and of the provincialism whereby different types of learning centers (centers focusing on content tutoring, writing, or strategies for learning; or that engage students using a particular pedagogy or model, or that serve a particular segment of the student body) while serving different aspects of the same mission, often do so in isolation from one another.

Moreover, zooming out to the broadest scale, the identity of learning centers is in flux. Learning centers grew out of the field of developmental education, but over time have grown to assume a much larger and more central role in colleges and universities. The model has grown, developed, and changed as it has absorbed new theoretical approaches, approaches to academic support, and models for peer-led learning. This rapid change, in combination with the fact that the scholarship of peer tutoring is distributed across multiple fields of professional and scholarly practice (education, learning center theory, writing center theory, supplemental instruction, and others) has resulted in widespread variation in how the term learning center is applied and understood on individual campuses, where it can be used to denote any of a very large number of types of programs. Within the field of learning center administration, and in this text, *learning center* refers to programs focused on peer tutoring. But learning center administrators operate within local realities, where the term might be understood in any number of different ways. It's important to understand them in working toward an organizational structure (both within and across centers at the same institution) that best serves the needs of students as well as in articulating a clear vision for the center that takes into account how stakeholders understand the center.

MODELS FOR LEARNING CENTERS

Changes over time in how learning centers are conceptualized have played out in different ways in different professional communities and different institutional contexts. This has resulted in a number of different models for learning centers that, although united by the same core pedagogy, reflect subtly different ways of understanding the work of the center and its relationship to other campus programs. Here we present five common (often overlapping) ways of conceptualizing learning centers:

• as a site for content tutoring,
• as a site for all peer tutoring,
• as a learning commons,
• as an academic one-stop, and
• as part of a larger center for teaching and learning.

As an LCA, understanding the model(s) that your center exemplifies is an important first step to understanding the center, its relationship to your campus, and the assumptions that may be driving how stakeholders perceive it.

Learning Centers as Sites for Content Tutoring

One common way of conceptualizing learning centers is as programs that provide peer tutoring for the content matter taught in academic disciplines. Learning centers construed in this way support students in doing homework, understanding concepts, memorizing information, learning languages, and preparing for quizzes and exams. They support general strategies for learning and student success, such as time management, critical reading, and note taking. It's fundamental to this view of learning centers that the center is defined essentially in opposition to writing centers. Writing centers have a strong sense of identity, unified by a robust and well-developed scholarship. Supporting writing across all areas of the academic curriculum, the modern writing center engages students over their writing (as well as, in many centers, public speaking) at a variety of levels (argumentation, style, organization, sentence-level concerns) and at all stages of the writing process (Boquet, 2001; Brooks, 1991; Ede, 1989; Harris, 1986; Lunsford, 1991; North, 1984). Learning centers, in this view, are essentially the home of everything else. At institutions with free-standing writing centers (an arrangement attested, according to the 2017 National Census of Writing, at 39% of 4-year institutions, and 32% of 2-year institutions), peer tutoring programs housed in learning centers tend to assume a complementary role, attending to those areas of the curriculum that the writing center does not cover.

A frequent and sometimes unintended consequence of this arrangement is a focus in learning centers on STEM disciplines. Because introductory science and mathematics courses are often prerequisite to courses of undergraduate study, and because they can be highly challenging, learning centers often (reasonably) design programming around the needs of the large numbers of students seeking support for chemistry, biology, and other areas of the natural and applied sciences. As a result, they can come to be associated by students with these disciplines. At the same time, the historical outgrowth of writing centers from departments of English, combined with the humanities being the most common area of training and academic affiliation for writing center administrators (Healy, 1995; Valles et al., 2017), can result in an association of writing centers among students associated with English, literary studies, and the humanities more broadly. These twin misperceptions (as much as learning center administrators and writing centers administrators alike work very hard to overcome them) can result in students from areas outside of STEM underutilizing learning centers, and students outside of the humanities underutilizing writing centers, despite the clear relevance of both skills for learning and skills for writing to all students, across all fields of study.

The largest downside to this understanding of learning centers is that it imposes an artificial distinction between learning centers and writing centers. Learning centers and writing centers tend to exist apart. As much shared DNA as may exist across all of these forms of academic support, as much as they may share values and face similar challenges, because these communities of practice have unique cultures, the tendency is not to communicate across the boundaries defined by them. Learning center and writing center professionals generally read different journals and go to different conferences, and although they grapple with many of the same questions and issues, they often do so in isolation from one another. The same drama tends to play out on our campuses, where a separation between writing centers and learning centers can create gaps in services. This is unfortunate, as many types of academic support (writing and presentations for the sciences, writing in non-English languages, learning strategies for the humanities and social sciences) tend to fall within this gap. Moreover, it imposes a separation where none would necessarily exist naturally for tutors and learners: writing and learning are inextricably intertwined, in every academic curriculum, and it's impossible to engage in either without the other.

This situation, in which a learning center exists in a complementary relationship to other forms of peer-led learning, can be exacerbated further by other programs that specialize in areas of the curriculum (centers focused on language learning, for example, or on mathematics). That puts programs identified on campus as "the learning center" in a highly constrained role, left either to duplicate other programming or to service the odds and ends that other programs don't address. To be clear, this is a highly limiting way to view learning centers, which should rather be defined capaciously to include all centers organized around peer-led learning. But for administrators within learning centers that exist in a complementary relationship with a writing center, it can be a reality, and addressing it is a highly important concern.

For learning center administrators within centers that complement writing centers or other types of peer tutoring programs, it's important to be proactive in creating a vision for the center, assuming agency in advancing a set of ideals and values rather than allowing the center to be passively defined in opposition to the more narrowly focused identities of other programs. It's also important to relate to these other centers as the natural allies that they are, rather than allowing a competitive, adversarial, dismissive, or simply distant relationship to emerge between programs. Gathering places on college campuses easily become discrete clubs, a dynamic that can be countered with programmatic collaborations, joint tutor trainings, shared celebrations, and other ways of finding common ground in the shared work of supporting students as learners.

Learning Centers as Sites for All Peer Tutoring

Another common way for learning centers to be construed is as programmatic and physical locations for all forms of peer tutoring, spanning a range of curricular areas and types of programming. Within a center conceived of in this way, a student might find peer support for biology, economics, French, writing, art history, and any number of other subject areas. Commonly, this support is organized in programs according to formats of support that correspond to communities of practice. Within a learning center conceptualized as the home for all forms of peer tutoring will generally be found, for example, writing centers and supplemental instruction (see chapter 3).

The profound advantage of such an arrangement is that it avoids unnecessary separation between programs that operate on very similar principles and theoretical underpinnings. It makes differences in programming that may not be intuitive for students (e.g., the support available through an SI session versus a drop-in lab) irrelevant, as they are both available through the same center. It allows for joint trainings for peer tutors across all areas of the curriculum, creating a campus-wide conversation on active and collaborative approaches to learning rather than disparate ones occurring in separate locations. It encourages students to take advantage of a variety of services by making it easier for students to use multiple services in ways that add to and enrich one another (e.g., seeing a content tutor to refresh on a concept, a math tutor to seek guidance on calculating and reporting a statistical analysis, and a writing tutor for assistance in generating an outline for a research report). And it makes collaboration between tutoring programs the rule rather than the exception, ensuring alignment between the various forms of peer tutoring available on a campus.

A possible disadvantage of this arrangement is that it can leave less room for the individual programs within the larger center to thrive, to themselves maintain a strong identity, and to gain a seat at the table in advocating for resources. For learning center administrators in such programs, the fundamental challenge is to ensure that each program within the center (or the specific program(s) under their purview) has sufficient autonomy to develop its own vision and approach, so that each can, in turn, enrich the center as a whole and still maintain a strong identity in the minds of campus stakeholders.

SILOING

Siloing is a common phenomenon in higher education, in which different parts of a college or university operate in relative isolation from one another, in ignorance of one another's efforts or even operating at cross purposes to one another. It's common within local landscapes for academic support to find widespread siloing of programs. Academic support initiatives formed at different points of time, emerging within different administrative partitions of an institution, and/or put in place by isolated grant initiatives often results in peer tutoring programs that may serve similar purposes but nonetheless operate in relative isolation from one another. Siloing is unfortunate for three reasons:

First, programming that fills the same function in two or more separate centers wastes resources. Because separate centers duplicate administrative structures, each independently providing the infrastructure to support peer tutoring, funds that would otherwise be available to provide academic support and meaningful employment for students end up being used instead to pay overhead costs. In an environment where funding for academic support is hard-won, and frequently a first target for budget cuts, this type of duplication of effort is hard to justify.

Second, siloing means that conversations about academic support that should be unified across the campus, involving everyone implicated by questions of peer-led learning, access to higher education, and supporting a diverse student body, take place in separate locations (and, inevitably, at different levels of quality) across campus. Planning can easily become disjointed rather than proceeding in unison toward a shared goal, and initiatives resulting from such isolated conversations may have an impact that is limited in scope, rather than on the institution as a whole.

Finally, and most troubling, siloing creates a barrier for students to access academic support. The more that students need to know about how to access support, the higher the bar is to do so. When accessing support is accomplished in different locations and in different ways for different aspects and areas of the curriculum, it becomes less intuitive and less accessible, resulting in students who would have benefited from tutoring not accessing it.

In some cases, it makes sense to maintain separation between peer tutoring programs, and ways exist to create healthy collaboration and communication between separate programs. But as a general principle, uniting academic support programs that have similar missions and outcomes under a single organizational structure will result in a far greater positive impact on students and on the institution than would be achieved by maintaining separation between them.

The Learning Center as a Learning Commons

The learning commons is a model for academic support that emerged from the scholarly ecosphere of libraries. An evolution of the information commons concept, the learning commons is a reconceptualization of the college or university library (or a specific space within it) as a locale where library resources, educational technology, and academic support services from around the institution converge to create a seamless, fully supported learning environment for students (Beagle, 2006; Bennett, 2003; Forrest & Hinchliffe, 2005; Franks & Tosko, 2007; Schader, 2007; Schmidt & Kaufman, 2007; Sinclair, 2007). With an explicit focus on incorporating programming within a shared space, driven by the needs of learners, without regard for organizational boundaries (between units, between libraries' and non-libraries' programming, between academic affairs and student affairs), learning commons often involve learning centers (as well as writing centers, and other forms of academically oriented student support) as prominent partners. The learning center and learning commons models, despite having their origins in two different times and two distinct professional and scholarly communities, have in common a focus on supporting students as learners, an academically oriented mission, and a premium on collaboration. As the two concepts have blended on campuses, among stakeholders for whom the difference between a "learning center" and a "learning commons" is understandably not intuitive, so too have they blended in the literature and professional communities of academic success. Since its emergence, the incorporation of the learning commons model represents one of the most important evolutions of the learning center concept.

The learning commons is a model emerging from both the changing role of libraries in higher education and the increasing integration of educational technology within the student experience. It's a model driven by the question of what the physical space of libraries is for, given the migration of informational resources toward online spaces, and it focuses on how resources can best be organized to support and drive the educational mission of institutions. Accordingly, for learning centers implemented on the learning commons vision, space is the organizing principle. A learning center, thus construed, is a physical location in which students are able to access multiple forms of academic support—tutoring, research librarians, IT support, mentoring, career counseling—within a space designed for collaborative learning and enriched with all of the informational and technological resources that a library is able to bring to bear.

In learning centers construed as sites for all peer tutoring, or as sites for content tutoring, generally, organizational structures provide coherence and unity of purpose, with a single learning center administrator overseeing all services; or with a team of individuals, each coordinating one aspect of a center's services, reporting to a director who provides leadership. In a learning commons model, on the other hand, programs offering support may represent a number of different organizational units. The physical environment of the commons—shared work implemented within a shared space—supports and facilitates collaboration. A learning center administrator operating within a learning commons environment may oversee peer tutoring within a larger commons that offers a variety of forms of support or a center in which peer tutoring is a central piece, but other forms of academic support that faculty or professional staff provide are available as well. In either case, a central concern for LCAs operating within a center predicated on the commons model is to facilitate collaboration, aligning discrete services in a way that feels seamless for students. It can also be important to advocate for peer tutoring as a model, ensuring that genuine peer-led learning is taking place even within an environment where professionals and faculty are also implementing services and working with partners who may not understand the value of peer tutoring (as opposed to instruction and mentoring by experts) as a form of academic support.

The Learning Center as an Academic One-Stop

The one-stop concept, which entered higher education from the business world as a way to streamline the student experience of accessing college functions such as financial aid, bursars' offices, and registration, has become a widespread model for implementing student-facing services in higher education. The one-stop model focuses on organizational efficiency and on customer service for students, placing related student services within a single, easily accessible location, often under the auspices of a single organizational unit (Burnett & Oblinger, 2003; Green, 2007; Kramer, 2003; Mesa, 2005; Nealon, 2007). It would be an anachronism to speak of the one-stop model as formative for learning centers, which developed from the outset as amalgamations of reading centers, study skills centers, resources centers, and other kinds of earlier iterations of academic support (Arendale, 2004; Christ, 1971). But the one-stop is both a relevant framework for understanding learning centers that combine a variety of academic support functions and a model that has played a role in shaping learning centers on many campuses as the one-stop approach has come to be applied to academic support services. The academic one-stop model for learning centers is in many ways similar to the learning commons model, in that it places a variety of support services in service of a single mission. Centers conceptualized as academic one-stops differ in that generally organizational structures, rather than space, create shared purpose. A model often associated with student affairs (as opposed to academic affairs), the one-stop center may occur in spaces other than libraries. It may also, although focused on peer tutoring, incorporate an array of services (e.g., testing services, academic coaching, offices of accessibility, career counseling, academic advising) that are implemented by professionals rather than by students.

A conceptualization of student support as customer service is a defining feature of the one-stop model, which often materializes in concierge-style service that focuses on creating a single point of intake for students and guiding them to the most relevant support for their needs. For students, this has enormous benefit: they have access to a variety of academic support services, but they don't bear the burden of understanding the difference between those services in order to access them. Students seeking/referred to support need only make it to the learning center. The center will line them up with the service(s) most suited to their needs.

For a learning center administrator overseeing or operating within a center implemented on the one-stop model, it's important to understand how peer tutoring fits in the suite of services that the center offers and how all of these services can best work together to create seamless support for students. It's also essential, because the burden of understanding the full complement of academic support services falls to the center rather than to the students, that the staff providing intake (whether professional or student, virtual or in-person) are empowered by robust training to ensure that students are connected to the services most relevant to their needs. It's also important, operating within a model generally focused on intake, to put a high premium on outreach, finding ways for the center to proactively engage the campus and for peer tutors to interact with courses, programming, students, and faculty *outside* the center.

DIVERSITY OF PROGRAMMING WITHIN LEARNING CENTERS

In 2016, Marcia Toms and David Reedy published the results of a large-scale survey of learning centers in the United States and Canada. In the responses from 211 institutions on the services provided with their learning centers, Toms and Reedy found tutoring, unsurprisingly, to be the most consistent service, offered at 98.1% of responding centers. The next most common type of programming, offered at 81.9% of centers, was study skills/learning strategies workshops/courses.

Variation is widespread beyond these two most frequent categories. Participating learning centers report offerings of supplemental instruction (57.4%), services for students on academic probation/warning (57.4%), services for students with disabilities (49.7%), computer lab (47.7%), organization of study groups (47.1%), academic coaching/counseling (47.1%), services for student-athletes (37.4%), peer mentoring programs (29.7%), academic advising (21.9%), assessment/placement testing of students (18.1%), first-year experience programs (16.1%), summer bridge programs (15.5%), TRIO programs (9%), personal counseling (5.8%), financial aid counseling (4.5%), and career services (4.5%). Some 32.3% of centers offer some service not included in the list above (the authors include "exam reviews, weekly course reviews, course-embedded tutoring, and large group drop-in tutoring" [p. 13] as examples).

Their results indicate that although peer tutoring and support for learning strategies form the relatively consistent core of learning centers' identities, learning centers can encompass an extremely broad spectrum of services offered both by student peers and by professionals. This widespread variation is consistent with the view of the learning center as a one-stop, where students can find, within a single location, a coherent suite of services to support them in their studies.

Peer Tutoring within Centers for Teaching and Learning

An emerging model is the combined center for teaching and learning, which places both faculty development and student academic support within a combined center. A stake in faculty development was present from the earliest moments in the history of learning centers. In 1971, Frank Christ described it as one potential role for learning centers to serve "as an information clearinghouse to update faculty in latest research and methodologies," acting to "ameliorate the learning situation in campus classrooms but also . . . effect good public relations between faculty and the Center" (p. 35). But only in recent years—at institutions as diverse as Princeton University, the University of New Mexico, Marymount University, Hobart and William Smith Colleges, and Stanford University—have centers for teaching and learning placed peer tutoring, workshops for faculty, and other services under the leadership of an executive director with a high institutional profile who has ultimate oversight of organizational units devoted to addressing both sides of the coin, teaching and learning.

Learning centers have moved, as a field, from an origin in developmental education toward a model of more broad relevance for every learner; and have grown and developed as active and collaborative approaches have become more widespread in higher education. At the same time, faculty development has moved away from a focus on educational technology toward a broader exploration of how instructors at the college and university level can teach in a way that centers students as learners and toward a more central role in institutions of higher education (Schroeder, 2011). The center for teaching and learning unites these two trends by synthesizing the two approaches, recognizing that learning is distributed across multiple sites, multiple layers, and multiple constituencies within an institution (Trammell & Bruce, 2008). The model has the inherent potential to more deeply enmesh peer-led learning in campus-wide approaches to teaching and learning, or to move it toward the periphery by inserting an additional link in the organization structures separating learning center administrators from the core leadership of the institution. The major advantage of a combined center for teaching and learning that incorporates both student- and faculty-facing programming is that it creates a single, shared conversation on pedagogy.

MISSION STATEMENTS

Learning centers—even new centers that exist within local histories—are conceptualized on their campuses based on stakeholders' understanding of what a learning center is. But learning centers don't just exist within institutional context. They affect them, operating in proactive ways to create more inclusive institutions, empower a culture of learning, and provide students with the means to succeed. Mission statements are an opportunity to actively assert the role of the center within the institution, taking an active hand in shaping how it is understood. Statements of mission should take into account the model (or models) that the center operates on, but also expand, modify, and otherwise move beyond them to proclaim the unique identity of the center and to articulate the values that inform the work that takes place within it.

Mission statements, and the process of creating them, set a vision for the center strong enough to shape how the program is being understood and how things function within it. They define the reason and purpose of the center, describing both what the center strives to do and how it will accomplish it. They connect the center to the overall mission of the institution, pointing to the value that the center adds to the educational enterprise of the college. Mission statements can feel extraneous on the ground, ideas that are easily forgotten in the chaos that is the day-to-day in learning-center administration. However, these statements serve as both inspiration and grounding. They help formulate goals that can then drill down to learning outcomes, which can then be assessed. When you begin to develop new programming or collaborate on projects, you can hold your ideas up to these statements to ensure that those ideas resonate with what your center aspires to be—which, in turn, assists in decision making about where to spend time, money, and resources strategically.

Program structure is intimately connected with the mission of learning centers. Learning center mission statements assert the role of the center within the institution. They also provide interior coherence, making the structure of the center transparent and articulating the logic of how the various programming initiatives within the center work together. For both students and professional staff, mission statements can provide a sense of shared purpose across the various programming initiatives (e.g., a supplemental instruction program, a writing center, an academic coaching program) that exist within a center, each adding a unique contribution (e.g., a focus on collaborative learning, or on writing as a tool for learning, or on learning strategies) to the overall mission of the center. Each individual peer program within a larger center can and should have sufficient autonomy to operate as a laboratory for a signature approach or set of pedagogies, which can then be transmitted out to contribute to the larger vision for the center. A strong mission is what provides this ability for each program within a center to operate as part of a greater whole rather than as an isolated initiative, and for the learning center as a whole to be a sum greater than its parts rather than simply a collection of programs. Ideally, each program within a center should have its own mission as well, connecting to the larger mission of the center but clearly staking out the unique approach, goals, pedagogies, and values of the program within it.

MISSION CREATION AS MISSION BUILDING

Creating a new mission statement or recrafting an outdated one is an incredible opportunity to promote buy-in from key stakeholders. For center staff and peer tutors, participation in creating a mission statement can also infuse a sense of shared purpose and a clear signal that their voices matter within the center, at the deepest level. For student users, faculty, and partner units, participation in developing a mission statement means fostering a sense of investment in the center's work. For LCAs, it provides an opportunity to reach out, introduce oneself, and demonstrate to stakeholders an interest in knowing them, and that their voice is valued. Everyone who participates feels not only proud of their contribution to the productive roadmap of the unit itself but an investment in its endeavors. Those who work within the unit are thrilled to understand the purpose behind the services they offer. Those who collaborate with the unit feel confident about what the unit can offer to the collaboration and how they will offer it. Having created a sense of shared investment in mission, it becomes far more effective to highlight these statements when explaining resource requests and reporting impact.

Involving the larger campus community is an iterative process of review and revision, involving progressively wider circles in providing feedback. Start with a polished draft mission statement that captures the core values, principles, approaches, and practices of the center (perhaps created through a collaborative process among the staff, students, and/or closest partners of the center). Begin successively distributing the mission to groups of stakeholders (tutors, partner units, faculty, administration), soliciting input. Redraft based on themes that emerge in feedback and move on to the next group of stakeholders. At the end of the process, share the center mission with the entire community, stressing the fact that it was created with input from every constituency. It's a lengthy process, but a mission in which people feel involved is immeasurably more powerful than one that reflects only the vision of a single author or small group, and the process of creating such investment can pay enormous dividends in creating good will for the center and for you as its administrator.

Although center mission statements allow tremendous room for variation, learning has common threads. In a 2009 report on a survey of learning centers at 142 colleges and universities, Truschel & Reedy report:

When reviewing the learning center mission statements posted on websites (N = 107), it became clear that most are committed to supporting and strengthening the academic experience of students. Several statements included terms to describe students' self-reliance, enhancing their self-regulation, and assisting students in developing academic and educational goals. There was also a focus on empowering students to reach their full academic potential and to provide a supportive learning environment. Learning centers also promoted retention through mission statement phrases such as "to provide individualized instruction to promote retention" or "to assist students in meeting demands of college level work." (p. 17)

Alignment with the broadest unifying principles of learning centers is an outstanding thing to capture within a mission statement (to this end, a review of mission statements at other learning centers, seeking those that resonate with one's own goals, philosophy, and approach, is an excellent first step in creating a mission statement). So, too, are the things that set your center apart: The way in which the model has been adjusted to fit within its particular institutional context, or is motivated by a unique driving vision.

For any one of the five common ways of construing learning centers presented here, the category contains countless variations, and beyond these any number of hybrids between, borderline examples of, and exceptions to them. The terrain of academic support within any one institution is frequently further complicated by the existence of multiple types of center, each representing a different aspect of the mission, and, in many cases, competing visions for learning centers. As LCAs, we may operate as administrators of centers that oversee all peer tutoring programs within an institution, as directors of centers that attend to one aspect of academic support, or as leaders of programs within a larger center. Regardless, our roles are fundamentally the same: to make sure that everything works together. To ensure collaboration, both within and across programs. And to set a vision strong enough to ensure that you shape how your program is understood and how it functions on your campus, rather than passively responding to the ways in which it may be understood.

QUESTIONS FOR PROGRAM ASSESSMENT

Organization of the Center

- Does the center reduce, as much as possible, what students need to know about accessing support in order to do so, by presenting academic support in a seamless, unified, centralized way to students?
- Does the center's organization take advantage of economies of scale and avoid wasting resources through duplication of efforts, by placing related peer-led programming within organizational structures that reduce the repetition of administrative structures?

- Does the center, either through the organizational structure, the physical space of the center, or some other means, ensure close collaborations between different aspects of academic support programming?
- Does the center create one centralized conversation about peer-led learning, pedagogy, and student success (as opposed to multiple, isolated conversations, distributed across campus)?

Mission

- Does the mission clearly articulate the goals and values of the center, providing a framework for decision making and assessment?
- Does the mission clearly articulate the practices and pedagogies the center uses, providing a clear picture for stakeholders of the work that takes place within it?
- Does the mission connect to the overall mission of the institution, indicating the role of the center within the college or university?
- Does the mission of the center provide a shared purpose and vision for each major program within it?
- Does each major program within the center itself have a mission, indicating the unique role of that program in fulfilling the greater mission of the center?

Chapter Three

Formats of Peer Tutoring

In peer tutoring, students engage their peers in learning interactions. Deflecting the role of expert and serving as guides and mentors, tutors provide insight on concepts, problems, and tasks based on their perspective as slightly more advanced learners within a curriculum. They foster collaborative learning and encourage learners to assume an active, reflective role in their own process of learning. Tutors challenge students to operate at the limits of their abilities and support them in doing so. They act as participants in shared inquiry and in the cocreation of knowledge. Peer tutors invite students to participate in the communities associated with fields of study and serve as attainable role models to the students they work with, demonstrating the strategies, attitudes, and tools that successful learners employ.

These goals and guiding principles of peer tutoring occur in every type of learning center and across every domain of academic inquiry. The actual form that peer tutoring takes, however, is incredibly diverse. Peer tutoring includes a large number of pedagogical approaches and formal models for peer-led learning. Several major approaches reflect different ways of thinking about the interaction between tutors and learners and include different goals for sessions. They can apply across any type of center and any disciplinary area. Other approaches to creating a typology of tutoring have been suggested (e.g., Olaussen et al., 2016; Topping, 1996; Whitman, 1988); the breakdown here is presented as a way to think through the possibilities for creating programming, considering the variation in programming that exists in learning centers, and weighing the advantages and disadvantages of these prominent approaches.

This chapter first provides four core types of peer tutoring—individual appointments, drop-in labs, workshops, and classroom-based tutoring. Then it turns to more specialized models for peer tutoring that have emerged within specific traditions. Within even a single center, a considerable range of models for tutoring can often be found (a diversity that is very much to the good for learners, as it creates multiple ways to engage with the center). In creating a suite of programming, an LCA is well-advised to consider the full diversity of approaches to peer tutoring (both general formats and specific models), including the unique strengths of each approach, and weighing how they best can be combined to form a whole greater than the sum of its parts.

INDIVIDUAL SESSIONS

In individual sessions, students meet one-to-one with tutors. Often the assumed default for tutoring, and the format that tends to align most closely with faculty and students' preconceptions about tutoring, individual sessions hold a time-honored place in centers for learning and writing (Cohen & Kulik, 1981; Harris, 1981; Hartman, 1990; Topping, 1996). Individual sessions are well-suited to an in-depth exploration of topics that represent barriers to students' progress within a course or curriculum or to review student work. Individual sessions are highly dialogic, involving a back-and-forth between the tutor and learner—often, this takes the form of tutors posing questions that help learners find their own answers. In an individual session, tutors act as collaborators, partners, and resources in the process of learning. Because individual sessions pair one tutor to one learner, they allow tutors to be maximally responsive to the unique needs of the learner with whom they are engaged, attending fully and intentionally to the identity, needs, and stage of learning of the learner. The very low tutor:learner ratio of individual sessions also allows tutors to create a plan for the interaction and implement it within a set time frame.

One of the primary perils of individual sessions is the dynamic that it can create between tutors and student users: with the student user in the role of learner, it can be easy for tutors to assume the corresponding role of expert. Asked a question by the student across the table, it's comfortable and natural for tutors—hired, after all, in part on the basis of their academic standing and understanding of the material—to answer it from a stance of knowledge and authority. The position of expert, however, is the least helpful stance for tutors to assume in working with learners, because it casts learners in the complementary role of novice. The goal of peer tutoring is to draw out and empower what students already know, rather than present knowledge to them. College students have no lack of educational venues in which they have a passive role. One of the most important points to stress to tutors is that learners should be full, active participants in individual sessions, and that the tutors' responsibility is to ensure that this takes place. Two often-cited guidelines are that tutors should strive to do no more than half of the talking in the session, and that learners should be holding the pencil/doing the work. Structures for knowledge are entrenched through using them and articulating them; learners in individual sessions should, as much as possible, speak and do (as opposed to listen and watch).

Individual appointments can be either scheduled or drop-in. Scheduled appointments make it possible for tutors to plan for sessions, because they know in advance when they will take place and how long they will last. Drop-in sessions have the advantage of greater flexibility, making it possible for learners to pop in with a quick query or stay for a longer period of time for a more in-depth project. Depending on how busy the center is, drop-in sessions can be stressful for tutors and pressure them to rush through sessions so that students who are waiting can be helped. Some students, in scheduling appointments, experience a calming sense of security in having done so, having a time and date they can point to on their calendars at which they will receive the support they need. Others may experience the extra step of having to make an appointment as an impediment or as a focus for anxiety. Having both options available (simply allowing learners to make immediate appointments if tutors are available), where possible, may make the center more accessible overall. Another consideration is that appointments make it easier to limit students' access to the center. Situations can and do develop in which learners make over-intensive use of tutors, for example, by staying in the center and working intensively with a tutor for several hours—a challenging circumstance for the tutor. Requiring appointments (and implementing policies such as no back-to-back appointments) makes it easier to head off such scenarios.

LEARNING CENTER MANAGEMENT SOFTWARE

Learning center/academic support center management systems are software platforms that organize, manage, and track the functions of learning centers. Most critically, such systems serve as the repository for tutors' schedules and specializations, creating availabilities that learners can access (e.g., by making a geography appointment during a shift that the LCA has entered for a tutor who is able to support geology courses). They also track student utilization of the center, recording information as students log in and out and storing it so that it can later be accessed in customized reports.

Such systems are expensive, but—provided that the system selected is a good fit for the center—very much worth the cost. Although it's possible to replicate some of these features with less expensive, more general-purpose software tools, software tools designed specifically for learning centers truly do offer a profound utility for LCAs, making it much easier and vastly less time-consuming to perform some of the most basic and recursive tasks of learning center administration. A number of dedicated software platforms for learning centers are available on the market at varying price points, each offering different options. Several extant early alert systems (see chapter 7) also offer some functionality for learning center management, raising the possibility of gaining free access to a license that the institution has already purchased.

Selecting an appropriate platform for your center has far-reaching implications: you'll spend countless hours interacting with it, so it's a choice you want to get right. Above all else, the learning center management software you select must fit your center: your formats of tutoring, the programmatic structure of your center, the way that you anticipate students interacting with the software, your intake procedures, and other aspects of the way your center is organized to implement its mission. Time spent carefully weighing the strengths and benefits of different systems as they pertain to your program is time extremely well spent: you never want to end up making pedagogical or programmatic decisions based on the constraints of the software system that you choose. As you vet programs, consider:

- **Ease of interface.** Both for student users and for the staff who engage with the program on a daily basis, the system should be intuitive, straightforward, and inviting. Clunky, off-putting interfaces are not only unpleasant, but they can waste time and even cause negative perceptions of the center.
- **Flexibility.** Ideally, a system will offer the adaptability to address a variety of scenarios and to meet changing needs as they arise. Often, flexibility and ease of interface act as counterpoints to one another, with an increase in one effecting a decrease in the other. Effective software design can, however, make even highly flexible systems relatively approachable.
- **Robust reporting functions.** Immediate access to aggregate data on students' utilization of the center is an absolutely essential function. Reporting functions should allow the LCA to quickly filter, sort, and export student utilization data according to any combination of date, student attributes, and service used.
- **Time clock and payroll functions.** It's extremely helpful (negating the need for an additional software system) if the software platform that manages tutors' availability also offers a simple, robust time clock feature that can also be used to make sure that employees are reporting for their scheduled and shifts and to create reports of tutors' hours worked for payroll purposes.
- **Integration capabilities.** If you wish to be able to link your center's management system to institutional data repositories (e.g., to be able to create reports filtered for student attributes such as race, GPA, or year in school), you'll want to ensure that this is a capability of the system, and that the company that created the system stands ready to support the integration process.

- **Data security.** Learning center management systems store sensitive, identifiable student information (an issue that is heightened if the system is integrated with other institutional systems), making it critical that they act as secure repositories. Make sure that the system you select has multiple layers of security in place to safeguard student data and, further, that it passes muster with your campus's IT department for the secure storage of legally protected student information.
- **Alignment with organization of the center.** For centers with multiple locations or programs, it's important to select a system that can handle these additional layers of complexity. Be sure to ask specific, pointed questions of representatives about how the system would best handle your program's specific organization.
- **Alignment with the center's formats of tutoring.** It's vital that the system you select can fluidly handle the tutoring formats your center uses without having to resort to clunky workarounds (e.g., many systems assume individual appointments as a default mode of tutoring, which may be problematic for centers that use drop-in formats). Make sure the system you select is built to facilitate your tutors' work.

Once you've selected a system, leave plenty of time to learn it, explore it, and set it up according to your center's needs: getting up and running with a learning center management system is a considerable process, taking several weeks at an absolute minimum for initial setup. Set aside time to engage with the system on a recurring basis, as well. Depending on the size and complexity of the center, allot a generous amount of time at the beginning of each term to input tutors and their schedules.

DROP-IN LABS

In drop-in labs (Cooper, 2010; DeFeo, Bonin, & Ossiander-Gobeille, 2017; Sanford, 2015), learners do the work of being a student—writing papers, doing homework, studying for exams, completing projects, reviewing notes, going over concepts—alongside other students working on the same thing, and tutors provide assistance as needed. Drop-in labs offer no appointments, nor do students wait to access them: they come during advertised hours and they get to work, staying for as short or as long as they like. Drop-in labs usually either focus on a single area of the curriculum, or they are divided into a number of areas (e.g., separate tables, with signs at each indicating the type of support available) with tutors in different areas focusing on different disciplines. Generally, students indicate that they would like the support of a tutor by raising a hand or through some other agreed-upon indicator.

Tutors also actively intervene, checking on students by offering input, asking questions, and generally ensuring that learners are making progress toward a goal. Collaborative learning is an essential aspect of drop-in labs. Because other students are present in the space as well, students are able to use their peers as resources and work together toward a deeper understanding of course concepts. In drop-in labs, tutors provide just enough support (in the form of questions, hints, tips, worked examples, alternate explanations of concepts, feedback, a critical eye, or other interventions as determined by the needs of the scenario) for learners to operate at the edges of their abilities. Through this scaffolding, students grow as independent learners, practicing skills in a supported environment that then become tasks that can be accomplished in other venues (e.g., alone in their dorm room, in class, or on an exam).

In individual appointments, the flow of student utilization of the center is capped by the format: when tutors are highly in demand, it may be more difficult to schedule an appointment, but the number of students who can use the center at one time is capped by the 1:1 ratio of tutors to learners. No such limits exist in drop-in labs, which can become extremely busy at times of peak use. Tutors in drop-in labs have to be comfortable working within what can be a loud, hectic environment. They also need to be comfortable using large influxes of students (driven by upcoming course deadlines) as pedagogical assets, engaging students in groups and getting students with similar material working together. Within a drop-in lab setting, tutors often shift roles toward being a facilitator of learning interactions between peers, setting up scenarios for collaborative learning rather than being direct participants. One of the most important advantages of the drop-in format is that it allows tutors to engage with learners as they are in the process of accomplishing academic tasks. In appointments, learners may feel that because they have limited time with tutors, they need to complete assignments before coming in (a factor that can become a hurdle to accessing tutoring). Appointments can then become a forum for talking about academic tasks rather than actually accomplishing them. In drop-in labs, where the open time frame means that students feel free to actually work, tutors can observe and intervene meaningfully regarding the strategies that learners are using in writing, problem solving, studying, reading, and learning.

Well-functioning drop-in labs can serve a large number of students in a highly effective way and set a culture for the center as a thriving place for learning on campus. It can take time, because drop-in labs align less closely with preconceptions of tutoring, to make an effective lab take hold. Students using the center tend to wait for help from tutors rather than get to work; and when they do get to work, they might assume they should do so quietly and independently. It takes time and clear direction (provided via signage and repeated prompting from tutors and center staff) to change the ways that students may approach tutoring.

For tutors, the same preconceptions may lead them to approach drop-in labs as sequential drop-in individual appointments, sitting down with one student and engaging them in a long one-to-one interaction before moving on to the next student. Tutor training should address the strategies of circulating throughout the lab, providing scaffolding for learners to move beyond their immediate hurdles so that they can continue working independently, getting students working together, and engaging students in groups. The at-times busy nature of drop-in labs can also create a challenging learning scenario for some learners. Although drop-in labs are highly effective in serving large numbers of students very effectively, it's important to provide alternate learning venues for students who may have a difficult time concentrating in a distracting environment, or who find it challenging to operate within a highly social environment.

WORKSHOPS

In workshop formats, peer tutors work individually or in small groups to facilitate sessions on topics of general or recurring interest for learners (Durkin & Main, 2002; Edwards & Thatcher, 2004; McKinley, 2011). A single well-timed workshop on a challenging topic within a curriculum can serve a widespread need in a student population. At the same time, work-shops make powerful and effective use of collaborative learning, leveraging the community of learners that emerges within a session as a forum for shared inquiry. Workshops may present, for students leery of any stigma they may associate with "tutoring," as a more welcoming and accessible form of academic support.

Workshops generally involve tutors (either working individually, or working in pairs or small groups to reduce the anxiety for presenters and create groups with complementary areas of strength/confidence) facilitating a session for a larger group of learners. The format of workshops in many ways suggests teaching, which can mean that tutors, seeking the most relevant models within their own experience for understanding the task in front of them, will often fall back on behaviors that instructors in their own classes have modeled, which may tend to place learners in a passive role. Workshops, as implemented through learning centers, are a form of peer tutoring and bear all the hallmarks thereof despite the superficial similarities to teaching.

It's important for peer tutors implementing workshops to understand that their role is to facilitate rather than teach, guiding learners through activities and discussions in which they have the opportunity to practice approaching and applying information in new ways, and in which everyone is able to participate in a mutually enriching process of collaborating toward a more meaningful understanding of a concept than any individual learner entered the room with. In practice, this generally means that workshops that peer tutors lead comprise a series of preplanned collaborative/active learning activities, perhaps beginning with a very brief outlining (with as much material as possible that learners, rather than facilitators, supply) of concepts that will frame the activity. The core pedagogies of tutors facilitating workshops are redirecting questions back to the group, posing questions and tasks to the group that invite students to contribute their own knowledge and experience to the collective, and activities that provide space for a back-and-forth of ideas and approaches among participants. Because of the structured, preplanned nature of workshops, it's important to provide tutors running them with time to plan and prepare.

Centers vary in the amount of latitude they provide tutors in developing and planning workshops. Creating and implementing a plan for a workshop can be a meaningful professional development opportunity for experienced tutors; some tutors may find it to be an overwhelming experience to be tasked with developing a plan for a session and may thrive more in implementing a workshop plan that the LCA or a tutor in a previous term has developed. The most successful workshops will always be those that are relevant to a large number of students; concepts and issues that come up on a recurring basis in tutoring interactions in the center are an ideal place to begin (accordingly, it's a good practice for LCAs to encourage tutors to suggest workshop topics based on trends they observe in sessions). Every campus is unique in the timing that works best for students, and it's wise to experiment with a variety of times and days of the week in seeing which offerings yield the most success in drawing attendees.

SAMPLE WORKSHOP TOPICS

The best workshop topics are those that will be relevant to a large number of students, either because they cover challenging core concepts in a class that many students take or because they cover academic skills that apply across a wide variety of courses. Workshops also provide an outstanding way to market the services of the center. Campus communications on upcoming workshops provide a steady stream of information to the campus on what services the center provides, creating a general awareness of the types of topics that fall within the purview of the center but of which students may not be aware. Sample workshops for a typical learning center might include:

- Mitosis in Action
- How to Study: What to Do When You're Sitting with Your Books and Notes
- Strategies for Dealing with Exam Anxiety
- Understanding Atomic Structure: Protons, Neurons, Electrons, and More
- Note Taking for Effective Studying and Retention
- Midterm Review for Economics 201: National Income, Output, Employment, and Inflation
- Time Management for Academic Essays
- Strategies for Memorization in Art History 101

Two common variations of workshops are exam reviews (in which a tutor leads a session on a review of topics that will be covered on an upcoming exam in a course) and study groups (in which tutors host regularly occurring sessions to decompress topics and problems being covered in the course and readings). Reviews and study groups are more emergent in nature than traditional workshops, with topics driven more by attendees' questions and needs than by a predetermined plan. Often, however, it's possible for tutors (perhaps working in collaboration with course instructors or TAs, or simply based on their own experience) to have an idea of which topics are likely to emerge and to prepare activities accordingly. Peer tutors facilitating exam reviews and study groups work with participants to set an agenda and help to keep things on topic. They support the group in negotiating ideas. They ensure that everyone is involved, providing all participants with the opportunity to articulate their understanding of concepts and, in doing so, reinforce what they know and identify gaps in their understanding. Above all else, they guide students through a process for collaborative study, supporting learners in developing skills for studying, for group learning, and for forming their own productive study groups.

CLASSROOM-BASED TUTORING

In classroom-based (or embedded) tutoring, peer tutoring is integrated with courses (Mullin et al., 2008; Soven, 2001; Spigelman & Grobman, 2005). Working in partnership with instructors and guided by the pedagogy of the learning center, peer tutors implement active, collaborative, learner-led pedagogies within the educational environment of the classroom. In time provided by the instructors, tutors can lead students in active learning breakout sessions, facilitate group work, and ensure that students understand assignments and concepts. They implement individual, drop-in, or workshop-based approaches that provide students in the course with time to decompress ideas, engage with the materials of the course in a different way, and apply strategies with support from peers. Often, tutors are available for individual or group consultations with students in the course outside of class as well.

Classroom-based tutoring has powerful benefits. For students in the course, it enriches the classroom experience, providing an additional level of support within the course as well as more opportunities for active and collaborative engagement. More broadly, it creates connections between the learning center and the classroom, extending the reach of the learning center into the curriculum itself as faculty develop collaborations with tutors and as they benefit from having active approaches to learning modeled for them. It can create stronger connections between the center and faculty, who will often become more knowledgeable about and invested in the center as a result of working closely with a tutor. Classroom-based tutoring also makes it as easy as possible for learners to access academic support, removing the onus for students to use the center by bringing the center to the spaces where they are already engaged in learning. In doing so, classroom-based tutoring functions as an ambassador program for learning centers, introducing students who may not otherwise ever have used the center to peer tutoring and building bridges from courses to the center.

Classroom-based tutoring is also fraught in the ambiguity that it can create in the role of peer tutors. Learning centers are student-led spaces where learners are in control of their own processes for learning. Classrooms are not. In entering classes and working in partnership with faculty members, peer tutors may find themselves in a different relationship to students in which learners may perceive them as authority figures or as agents of the instructor, department, or curriculum. Complicating this picture, instructors working with peer tutors in the classroom may not understand the clear difference between graduate or undergraduate teaching/instructional assistants (who work for academic departments, supporting faculty as teachers, and often play a role in assessing student performance) and peer tutors (who work for the learning center supporting students as learners, and who absolutely must play no role whatsoever in assessing student work at the risk of completely undermining the peer tutoring relationship). It's essential in implementing classroom-based tutoring programs to adequately invest time in training both peer tutors and faculty on the role of tutors in courses and to be prepared to intervene in situations in which tutors may receive pressure from faculty to go beyond their role as peer tutors. A common practice is to have faculty sign off on a contract—serving as both a tool for education and a useful document to draw on in situations where misperceptions of the role of classroom-based tutors arise—that clearly articulates the role of embedded tutors in courses.

ONLINE TUTORING

In online sessions, peer tutors and learners engage with one another through a digitally mediated environment. One advantage of online tutoring is that it offers an alternate means of accessing the services of the center for those who are constrained in their capacity to do so (e.g., due to a disability that makes visiting the center in person impractical, to operating at a large physical distance from campus, or to a work/family schedule that makes accessing the center during its regular hours impractical). Increasingly, however, online tutoring is an option that many take advantage of due simply to convenience or to personal preference. Online tutoring isn't an alternate format so much as an alternate medium for tutoring: any format or model for tutoring outlined in this chapter can take place in either physical or online venues, and it can be implemented through a variety of platforms (interactive whiteboards, text chat, learning management systems, and many others).

It's important to remember that online learning has no one "right" approach. Online tutoring interactions can differ in a variety of ways (e.g., the extent which they use written text, graphic interfaces, audio components, and visual components). No specific combination of these ingredients offers the best experience for users or the most ideal conditions for learning. The relative merits of different platforms and approaches can only be assessed in relation to a particular learning scenario. In making choices on the forms of online support your program offers:

- **Consider both synchronous and asynchronous approaches.** More synchronous approaches, in which communication takes place in real time (e.g., video chat, instant messaging), have the strength of tracking more closely with face-to-face tutoring. More asynchronous approaches, in which the format of communication introduces a significant delay between messages (e.g., e-mail, message boards), have their own pedagogical advantages, allowing for a level of planning and collaboration that is otherwise challenging to attain. Online tutoring sessions do not have to replicate face-to-face tutoring to be effective—indeed, asynchronous approaches in some ways take better advantage of the online environment.
- **Balance flexibility with the need to create a simple learning environment.** Platforms for online tutoring can offer an incredible array of tools for tutors and options for learners. For a learner seeking support, however, such flexibility may well be more intimidating than welcoming. Worse, cognitive resources that could otherwise be applied to the academic task at hand may have to be redirected to navigating an unfamiliar environment. Depend as much as possible on tools and technologies that are already familiar to students on your campus. Where this isn't possible, provide as much opportunity as possible for learners to become comfortable with the environment before engaging with a learning task.

- **Give online learners multiple ways to engage with the center.** Students seeking online academic support do so for a variety of reasons. For those learners for whom accessing the center online is a better option than in-person support, strive to provide a variety of ways to do so (e.g., both asynchronous and synchronous, both appointments and drop-in, both text-based and video-based). As with brick-and-mortar learning environments, it's important to provide learners with a variety of meaningful options for engaging with academic support and to provide tutors with a variety of tools for supporting learning in online environments.
- **Provide robust training for peer tutors on engaging with learners online.** Online environment entails considerable pedagogical opportunities. In addition to supporting accessibility and providing additional options for accessing support, online tutoring offers the powerful advantage of providing tutors and learners with rapid access to online tools and resources to support disciplinary learning. Online environments also offer unique challenges, most critically the potential absence of cues that make interpersonal communication function more smoothly (as well as making it easier for tutors to attend to learners' emotional states). In order to both take advantage of the benefits and mitigate the liabilities of online environments, it's important that tutors have specialized training in online tutoring. Sanford (2020) offers guidance for tutors (as well as LCAs) in considering the relative merits of different forms of online tutoring and guidance for engaging learners within them.

A growing number of companies provide online tutoring for institutions through a proprietary platform that the company's own private tutors staff. For learning centers, entering into such an agreement provides the opportunity to focus time and energy on in-person services and avoid the task of developing an online suite of programming. It should be noted, however, that the peer tutoring model does not sanction outsourcing of online tutoring: the tutors that private companies employ are not the peers of students at your institution, they do not have direct knowledge of your local curricula, and they are not trained according to the same standards as your tutors. Developing and implementing a homegrown suite of online services takes time, but it will result in a service far more in line with the center and its values. Further, it's an opportunity to gain familiarity with tools and pedagogies that can, in turn, enrich the entire center.

In addition to these four overarching formats for tutoring, a number of specialized models for tutoring often exist as discrete programs within learning centers. Although every disciplinary area has its own particular concerns that unfold in tutoring scenarios, these are unique in that they reflect a specific approach to tutoring associated with a field of scholarship and professional practice.

SUPPLEMENTAL INSTRUCTION/PASS

Supplemental instruction (SI), commonly known outside of the United States as peer-assisted study sessions (PASS), is a highly structured model for academic support that incorporates elements of both workshop and classroom-based tutoring. (SI/PASS is sometimes described as an alternative to peer tutoring, but this can be the case only when peer tutoring is construed in the narrowest, most dated sense as being limited to individual consultations.) The core insight of the supplemental instruction model since its inception in 1974 has been to attach support to challenging courses rather than to at-risk students, which has the effect of disproportionately impacting those students most in need of assistance while avoiding the stigma that can be associated with remedial programming (Blanc, DeBuhr, & Martin, 1983; Martin, 1980; Martin & Hurley, 2005). SI leaders attend the class they support, where they make themselves known as a resource to students, model ideal student behavior for their peers (e.g., taking notes and asking questions), and become familiar with the course assignments as well as the instructor's specific approach to the material. SI leaders then facilitate review sessions outside of class, focusing on structured active and collaborative group activities that provide students with an alternate way to engage with the course material. SI leaders generally meet regularly with instructors to strategize support for the course. A common extension of the SI/PASS model is for leaders to hold office hours in which they are available for individual consultations with students in the course.

SI/PASS is a model with an enormous amount of associated structure (SI programs are certified in the United States by the International Center for supplemental instruction at the University of Missouri at Kansas City, in Canada at the University of Guelph, in Europe by the European Centre for SI-PASS at Sweden's Lund University, in Australia at the University of Wollongong, and in South Africa at Nelson Mandela University, all offering training for administrators of SI/PASS programs). Although certified programs follow a relatively strict set of criteria, programs inspired by or based on the model without strictly following it are common as well. The consistency of the SI model makes it highly assessable, and a very large body of research points to the success of SI/PASS in increasing student success along a variety of parameters (Burmeister, Kenney, & Nice, 1996; Chilvers, 2016; Coe, McDougall, & McKeown, 1999; Etter, Burmeister, & Elder, 2000; Forester, Thomas, & McWhorter, 2004; Kochenour et al., 1997; Mason & Verdel, 2001; Ning & Downing, 2010; Spaniol-Mathews, Letourneau & Rice, 2016; Yockey & George, 2000).

LEARNING STRATEGIES

Support for learning strategies (also known as study skills) covers academic habits that overarch individual courses and contribute to students' academic success across *all* of their courses. Support for note taking, time management, critical reading, problem solving, studying, test taking, and other academic habits can be life-changing for students and transformative for institutions, because it engages directly with students' ability to operate as independent learners (Hartman, 1990; Ishiki Hendriksen et al., 2005; Jarrett & Harris, 2009). Engaging students over learning strategies is a deeply important part of a center's toolkit for supporting students in the first year, when they are recalibrating the academic habits that they cultivated in high school for the new challenges of life at a college or university (Chester et al., 2013; Durkin & Main, 2002; Smith, Walter, & Hoey, 1992). It's also critical for first-generation to college students, who didn't grow up with family lore of college life and who don't have family support that can speak to basic strategies for succeeding in college (McConnell, 2000; Stebleton & Soria, 2012; Strayhorn, 2006).

Tutoring for learning strategies can take place in a few different ways (or any combination thereof). First, support can be implemented through a dedicated tutor, or team of tutors, who focus exclusively on learning strategies as their content area and engage with students over the strategies that they bring to their studies through the tutoring formats above. Workshops are a particularly common way for centers to engage with students over strategies for learning. Second, learning strategies can be integrated with tutoring for all content areas that the center serves through tutor training, with tutors trained on effective strategies for learning and on recognizing situations in which it may be appropriate to focus on learning strategies rather than content. Third, learning strategies can be engaged with through peer mentoring programs. Though not strictly a form of peer tutoring (peer tutoring and peer mentoring are the two core pedagogies that occur within the larger field of peer-assisted learning [Loots, 2009; Topping & Ehly, 2001]), peer mentoring is a common programming component in learning centers. In peer mentoring programs, less experienced students are paired with more experienced students with whom they meet regularly, developing a relationship. Alongside helping mentees to feel a greater sense of engagement and belonging within the institution, the transmission of strategies from successful students to students in need of such strategies is a cornerstone aspect of mentoring programs.

However support for learning strategies is implemented, training is essential. In working with students, tutors should have the benefit of the robust body of literature on effective research-based practices for learning. Training in which tutors reflect on their own strategies for learning, or consider how to recognize learners who may be having issues with learning strategies, are essential. In addition, tutors often find it challenging to transition sessions away from content and toward learning strategies, as learners who are focused on their immediate academic goals may not understand the importance of doing so. Training sessions that focus on developing and practicing strategies for shifting sessions toward academic habits are extremely valuable support for tutors.

WRITING TUTORING

It's common within learning centers construed as sites for all peer tutoring, as learning commons, or as one-stops (see chapter 2) to find writing tutoring as a program or service offered within the larger context of a learning center that offers a variety of forms of support. This is an arrangement with much to say for it. When learning centers and writing centers are combined within a single program, it heads off territorialism and fosters collaboration. It allows for a shared tutor training program based on the core pedagogical principles of peer tutoring that apply across both writing and content tutoring and for learning centers to engage with areas of the curriculum where the bulk of assessment takes place via writing. On the other hand, it's critical for LCAs overseeing writing tutoring programs to be cognizant that a robust community of scholarship and professional practice is associated with writing tutoring.

In many ways it is beneficial for writing and content tutors to work closely together and to train alongside one another on the core principles of peer tutoring. But it's also critical for writing tutors to have access to the large field of relevant scholarship and specialized training materials for writing tutoring and to meet periodically as a separate group to discuss the unique challenges inherent to tutoring writing. Doing so can result in enriching the center overall. Many of the ideas and tensions that have been explored in-depth within the scholarship of writing centers—foundational ideas such as directive versus nondirective tutoring (Clark, 1988; Shamoon & Burns, 1995) and a focus on process rather than on the final product (Bruffee, 1984; Lerner, 1999), and in more recent scholarship, positioning centers as sites for allyship toward marginalized groups on campus (Denny, 2010; Green, 2018) and for supporting linguistic diversity (Rodby, 2002; Suhr-Sytsma & Brown, 2011)—are profoundly relevant for learning centers more broadly, and it's very much to the good to have a team of writing specialists who can disseminate this research to the larger group.

Within writing centers, the tradition of individual consultations is strong, but it's by no means necessary for writing tutoring to take place in individual appointments—writing tutoring has been successfully implemented in all of the formats for peer tutoring outlined above.

DESIGNING A PROGRAMMING SUITE

In designing (or redesigning) a menu of offerings for students who use the center, consider two important factors. First, provide as many options as possible for learners. The way in which this principle will be implemented will vary widely for different types and sizes of center, ranging from ensuring that a given topic can be accessed both in-person or online, to having multiple teams of tutors each specializing in a different pedagogical approach. But to whatever extent is possible, given the scope of the center, providing a variety of options in tutoring formats, tutoring topics, and combinations thereof provides multiple ways for students to access the center, making the center relevant to the broadest possible cross-section of the student body while at the same time being mindful of the needs of individual learners. Within the context of your center, this may mean that students have access to content tutors, writing tutors, and learning strategies tutors for a given course, depending on their current needs. It may mean that individual and group formats of tutoring are both available, providing multiple options for students who feel varying levels of comfort in social scenarios. In whatever way is reasonable and realistic to create them for your center, options empower students by providing them with meaningful choices, fostering a sense of agency in their own journey as learners.

Second, create teams that foster a sense of specialization among the tutors. Such an organization can take place according to disciplinary areas (e.g., language tutors, writing tutors, natural sciences tutors), tutoring format (e.g., supplemental instruction leaders, drop-in lab tutors), or some combination of the two. But particularly in larger centers, the separation of peer tutors into teams allows each team to function as a mutually supportive cohort and as an incubator for pedagogies and approaches that are cultivated within a team but can then be spread to enrich the center as a whole. The separation of tutors into programs also creates a space for tutors to explore, in trainings, areas of scholarship that are uniquely relevant to their work with students (e.g., second language acquisition for language tutors, the scholarship of SI/PASS for supplemental instruction leaders).

Various services/programs are implemented within a center. Each contributes to the overall identity of the center, but each should also have a clearly understandable identity that can be quickly and easily articulated to campus. It's easy, as an LCA running a learning center or a program within a center (having spent time immersed in thinking about learning centers and studying aspects of academic support programming), to fool oneself into thinking that the differences between the various formats, modes, and disciplinary areas of tutoring are intuitive. It's essential to have a clear vision for the unique aspects of each program within the center and a short, lucid explanation for every service available to students that makes it clear to students why they would choose one over another, to faculty and staff how to make referrals to them, and to administrators what the range of programming is that exists within the center. If a program and the role it plays within the center can't be explained clearly in a very short amount of time, it will likely never have a clear identity on campus.

No one best way exists to organize learning center programming, because every learning center is situated within a unique institutional context, arises from a unique history, and is responsive to the unique needs of the student population that it serves. Ultimately, it's possible to organize programming within learning centers in as many ways as there are learning centers. What's important is that a diversity of programming types exist, and that the types of programming that exist within the center complement one another, each speaking to a different aspect of supporting learners in succeeding and thriving within the academy.

QUESTIONS FOR PROGRAM ASSESSMENT

- Do all formats of tutoring place students in an active role in the session?
- Do tutoring formats involving more than one learner take advantage of collaborative pedagogies, using tutors at least to some extent as facilitators of interactions between learners?
- Do the programming options offered within the center allow students who prefer a quieter, less distracting environment to access support?
- Do the programming options offered within the center allow students who prefer an active, social learning environment to access support?
- Do the programming options offered within the center provide ways for the center to handle large influxes of students, particularly at times of heavy utilization?
- Do the programming options offered within the center provide a way for students to use the center who may associate a sense of stigma with using "tutoring"?
- Within the tutoring formats provided by the center, are there opportunities for tutors to engage with students who are in the process of working/ learning/studying/writing, so that they can observe and engage with learners' processes in these tasks?

- Is the role of peer tutor clearly delineated from the role of TA or under-graduate assistant (in all tutoring formats, but especially classroom-based tutoring), with tutors serving the needs of learners rather than faculty and playing no role in assessing student work?
- Does the programming in the center address learning strategies, either as a dedicated program or as a prominent but integrated part of all services?
- Does the center provide, for each major disciplinary or content area, a variety of formats of tutoring that offer meaningful options for students?
- Does the arrangement of programs or services within the center allow for teams of tutors to develop a sense of specialization in particular methods, pedagogies, or approaches to tutoring?
- Is the variety of programming options within the center presented to students and faculty in a way that is intuitive and makes it clear the basis on which a learner might choose one service over another?

Chapter Four

Students as Employees

The positive change that radiates out from learning centers is a function of beneficial attitudes, strategies, and behaviors being transmitted between learners, like links in a chain, as students interact with one another. The beginning of this chain, and the starting point for all of the beneficial influence that learning centers have on populations of students, is the tutors. Hiring students with the skills and aptitudes to serve as peer tutors and retaining them so that they can contribute to the center in progressively more meaningful ways is pivotal to the success of a center in making a true difference within the institution it serves.

In order to accomplish these goals, the center needs to be a good place to work for the students who fulfill its mission. A positive culture of employment—one in which student employees feel valued and included—provides a framework for peer tutors to grow as educators. It cultivates the conditions for students to experience the academic and professional benefits of serving as peer tutors. It fosters a sense of structure and mutual accountability among the tutors. And it allows the center to benefit from the vision that peer tutors bring as individuals with unique strengths and as bright students who have critical insight to offer based on their perspective as learners within the curricula they support.

HIRING

Creating an effective hiring process that ensures a strong student staff is one of the most indispensable functions of an LCA. Tutor training and creating a strong culture of employment build on the strong foundation laid by effective hiring, ensuring that students hired as tutors have the support to succeed in their roles. Nothing is more important, however, in creating an effective, impactful center than hiring students as tutors who have the right strengths to support students in their growth as learners and in creating a team of tutors who collectively are able to respond to a broad variety of student backgrounds and needs.

Success as a college student—as learners, writers, problem solvers, and critical thinkers in the disciplines—is an important attribute for tutors. One of the essential services that tutors provide is modeling the behaviors and strategies that successful students employ. It would be challenging for tutors to provide this modeling without having attained a degree of success in their own studies. Grades are one way of gauging students' degree of success as students, and a common practice in many centers is to require a transcripted grade above a certain threshold (e.g., a B or better) for any course students will be tutoring, as well as an overall GPA above a specific level (e.g., 3.0). Another is taking advantage of faculty as allies in hiring. As experts in their fields, faculty are invaluable in speaking to students' degree of comfort with course concepts.

FACULTY REFERRALS

Faculty are invaluable partners in hiring tutors. Faculty know the students in their classes and programs and have firsthand knowledge of students who have a strong grasp of the material, who are particularly conscientious in meeting their obligations as students, or who may be naturally emerging as leaders among their peers. Gathering faculty input on tutor hiring is an outstanding way both to recruit tutors to the center, and to create investment in the center among the faculty. Gathering nominations from faculty on students from their courses and majors who they feel would make good candidates for positions as tutors is one easy and helpful way to involve faculty in hiring, while also creating a large pool of possible tutors. Many centers also require a letter of recommendation from a faculty member as a part of a student's application for employment with the center, or as a final step before hiring.

As valuable as faculty nominations and referrals can be, it's also important to take them with some reservations. Faculty who aren't familiar with peer tutoring pedagogy will generally refer their best students as tutors. Although knowledge of course material is one important qualification for tutors, it's far more important that tutors have empathy for the student who is struggling to master the material—often, the best potential tutor is the student who worked very hard for a B, as opposed to the student who has an intuitive grasp of the content of the course and coasted to an A. Clearly communicating to faculty what you are looking for in tutors is one important strategy. Collecting a list of nominations, rather than one or two, is also an effective tool, as it provides you with flexibility.

It's important not to weight faculty referrals so heavily that choices on hiring are effectively yielded to faculty. Selecting the right tutors to staff the center is one of the most critical ways you can shape the identity and culture of your center, and it's important that you reserve the right to make choices that will create an effective and diverse group of tutors, even when it means hiring tutors other than those who were referred.

As important as content knowledge is, however, it's far from the most important factor in hiring tutors. One of the most common mistakes novice LCAs make is in using student success as the sole, or even as a leading, criterion for selecting tutors. Effective tutors are students who are able to understand the challenges of students who are struggling in their studies. Often, the student who was able, by virtue of outstanding preparation or innate ability, to breeze through a course with relatively little effort is least equipped to help peers succeed. The student who had to struggle for a grade, even if that grade is perhaps a B rather than an A, is generally more aware of what is challenging about the material and of strategies for overcoming that difficulty, and is able to meet learners currently engaged in the struggle to overcome similar challenges with patience and empathy. The most important attributes in potential peer tutors are clear communicative ability, interpersonal warmth, a capacity for growth, and a willingness to face uncomfortable situations. In hiring tutors, above a minimum threshold of student success in a course or major, all of these factors should outweigh academic achievement.

Breadth is also an important lens for considering potential tutors. In hiring, the goal is to create a group that, collectively, can respond to as broad a variety of student needs as possible. Generally, a student who is able to support a *curriculum*—a variety of courses within a major or course of study, through at least the introductory level and perhaps beyond—is more valuable as a potential tutor than a student who is able to support only a specific course or two (for this reason, many centers do not, as a policy, hire first-year or undeclared students). Similarly, a student who has the ability to tutor a variety of high-need courses across the curriculum is in many cases a better candidate than one who is only able to tutor courses within a single department. In a center of any size, much of what an LCA does day-to-day is to align the resources of the center with the needs of students. The greater the collective flexibility of the tutoring staff, the easier this task will be.

INTAKE SPECIALISTS

One student employment role to consider in staffing the center is that of students who can serve as intake specialists (or student resource representatives, or welcome workers, or whatever name is resonant for your program) to staff the front desk(s) of the center.

Student intake is vital to making the center a welcoming and inclusive space, to connecting students to the appropriate support, and to gathering accurate information on student usage. It can be understandably challenging, however, for tutors who are engaged in learning interactions to make intake a priority. Student employees who are fully dedicated to the role of intake specialists, on the other hand, can give their full attention to greeting and welcoming learners as they enter the center, orienting them to the various formats of tutoring, logging them in and out, answering their questions on hours and availability, creating appointments, and referring students to other campus academic support services as appropriate.

Hiring students as intake workers isn't possible for every center, but where it is, it's a good investment. With training and support, intake specialists can play a critical role in directing students to the appropriate support, whether that support exists within the center (e.g., a writing tutor, a content tutor, a learning strategies tutor) or in another location (e.g., a research librarian, faculty office hours, the IT desk). The position also creates an employment opportunity for students who may be good future prospects as tutors but have not yet progressed through enough of the curriculum to qualify.

Finally, embodied diversity is an essential consideration in hiring tutors. If tutors are to serve as role models for students using the center, it's critical that *every* student who enters the center can see students who look like them. The first step in creating a learning center that is fully welcoming to every student on campus is to create a team of tutors that represents, to the greatest extent possible, the full range of identities present on campus. Embodied diversity is important across a wide spectrum of difference, but it is particularly critical to be attentive to the representation of underrepresented minority (URM) students. Systemic inequity, and the high association of academic achievement with socioeconomic status, often result in white students performing at a level above their URM peers on traditional indexes of academic achievement (Anderson & Kim, 2006; Greene, Marti, & McClennney, 2008; Huang, Taddese, & Walter, 2000; Shapiro et al., 2017; Spenner, Buchmann, & Landerman, 2004). Full representation of URM students within the center, and on each team of student employees within the center, means hiring practices that are proactive in inviting URM students to apply and place explicit value on racial diversity.

INTERVIEW QUESTIONS

The questions you ask tutors should reflect the particular values of your center and the traits you seek in tutors. It can be helpful, however, to have a basic set of questions as a starting point. Here is a list of potential questions, based on our experience interviewing students as potential peer tutors.

- Why do you want to be a tutor? How does this position fit with your goals?
- Could you tell me about a moment of crisis that you've experienced in your own academic career? How would that experience affect your approach as a tutor?
- Have you ever used the learning center? What was that experience like for you?
- Why is peer tutoring important?
- Think of a concept that comes easily to you or was easy for you to learn. How would you go about helping someone else for whom the concept is not intuitive to understand it?
- What does effective student leadership mean to you?
- What is the value of diversity in higher education? As a peer tutor in this center, how would you work to support a diverse student body?
- What unique strengths (based on your background, studies, work history, or anything else) would you bring to this position?
- What are some common challenges that students in your major face? As a tutor, how would you help students overcome them?
- Why might a student be nervous about using tutoring? How would you help them overcome that barrier so that they feel comfortable and want to come back again?
- Talk about a time when you received helpful support from a peer. What made it helpful?
- What is your favorite way to learn something new? How would you incorporate that into a tutoring session with a student user?

Suggested Process for an Annual Hiring Cycle

Hiring is one of the most critical, most time-consuming, parts of learning center administration. With some planning, it's possible to collect a large pool of potential tutors, avoid a last-minute crunch, and extend offers to great students before other campus programs grab them. Most centers have a large hiring push in the lead-up to the fall semester, so that the freshly minted staff of tutors can be assembled for training at the beginning of the academic year. This plan assumes such a cycle, but it can be modified according to the needs of individual programs. In your hiring cycle, be sure to account for the sometimes-significant time delay between offering a position to a student and receiving a go-ahead from student employment for them to begin working.

Throughout the Year: Create a Running List of Potential Tutors

As you and others in the center come into contact with students who have the attributes of potential tutors, take note of them. The center itself is the best place to find students who are aware of the benefits of peer tutoring, who understand what it is to work hard to succeed, and who are taking agency in their own journey as leaders. In the day-to-day of center administration, make notes as you come across students who may be developing toward a potential student leadership role.

Six Months Out: Create All Hiring Materials

Craft/revise job descriptions for all student employment roles. Decide what application materials you will require and create instructions for applying. Before gearing up for hiring, dedicate time (individually, or as a staff) to considering your postings. Do they communicate a compelling vision for why students would want to be tutors? Do they describe what the center values in tutors? Will the type(s) of student that you hope will apply see themselves as potential candidates, based on what's described in the posting? Revise accordingly.

Consider as well what application materials you will require: transcripts? A résumé? A cover letter? A letter of recommendation? A sample of academic work? Remember that students are busy. The harder it is for students to complete an application, the fewer will do so. It's also possible to request more materials later in the process (e.g., after interviews).

Five Months Out: Create a Public Call for Nominations

Invite tutors, students, faculty, and staff to nominate students for positions as peer tutors and use every available channel of communication (e-mail listservs, social media accounts, flyers, etc.).

Include a description of the qualities that the center values in potential tutors. A call for nominations is an opportunity to create widespread community involvement in and awareness of the center while also gathering a large list of potential candidates. At this stage, casting a wide net is desirable— filtering will come later in the process. Don't forget the current tutors, who know better than anyone the attributes of a good tutor and who are deeply connected to student communities, as a resource in gathering nominations. Self-nominations should be encouraged as well.

Four Months Out: Assess Your Hiring Needs

Establish the budget for hiring tutors and determine which positions are needed. Survey the current tutoring staff to see who plans to return to employment in the following academic year. In this critical step, you're determining which positions you aim to fill during hiring so that all applicants can be vetted to fill specific spots, rather than simply as tutors.

This is also a good moment to consider whether any individuals on the current staff will not be invited back for employment the following year.

Three Months Out: Post and Advertise

Advertise the postings widely, inviting everyone interested to apply. Using the list you received in the previous step, e-mail students to let them know that they've been nominated and invite them to apply.

Hold hiring fairs for students to learn about employment and meet current tutors. The list of nominees you've collected becomes an asset at this stage, as you're able to reach out to a robust, targeted list of candidates with an invitation to apply. Make sure that students know that they were nominated, that the nomination in itself is an honor, and that they are specially invited to apply based on their nomination.

Hiring fairs (ideally staffed by current tutors) provide an opportunity to create more awareness of the postings, and for students who may be interested in applying to seek clarification about reservations, questions, or concerns in a low-stakes venue. When hiring fairs are held in the spaces of campus partners (ethnic centers, athletic programs, academic units), they can help with outreach to specific groups of students.

Two Months Out: Vet Applicants

Make decisions, based on applications, on which applicants should be considered for interview. At this stage it's useful to separate applicants into three categories: those who should definitely receive an interview, those who should definitely not be hired, and those who should be held in reserve. This final group can be returned to fill particular needs in the hiring roster later in the process.

One Month Out: Interviews and Final Decisions

Interview all applicants who were selected for finalist status and extend offers for employment based on the spots available, along with information on employment and orientation. Politely notify other students that they were not selected at this time. If desired, notify students that they have been placed on a waiting list for spots that become available, or invite them to apply again in future hiring cycles.

At this stage of interviewing, you already know the students' credentials. Use interviews to look for the intangible qualities that make students good tutors: empathy, warmth, clear communicative ability, and an understanding of what it is to struggle academically. Remember, for students you hire, the interview is your first opportunity to shape how they understand the center and their role within it. Be sure to set a welcoming tone and take the opportunity to articulate a strong vision for the center and for peer tutoring.

CREATING A POSITIVE CULTURE OF STUDENT EMPLOYMENT

Peer tutors have direct knowledge, rooted in recent and firsthand experience, of how the students we serve are experiencing the curriculum. They have insight into the literacies, values, and attitudes of students entering the academy. A center that embraces input from tutors, allowing room for their voice and vision within the center in palpable ways, is a far better place to work for the tutors within it. It is also a center that is much more responsive to the students it serves. Learning centers are driven by a philosophy that advances students, rather than professional educators, as agents of change and of pedagogical excellence. It's incumbent on us to create cultures of student employment that follow from this philosophy as well, centering tutors by supporting the work they do and providing them with opportunities to serve as leaders not only among their peers, but also within the center itself.

LEARNING CENTERS AS ETHICAL EMPLOYERS

Ethical employment practices in any workplace ensure that workers are treated with fairness and respect. In the context of a learning center, ethical employment also means honoring the student-first ethos of the center and protecting the conditions that make it possible for peer tutors to excel as both students and professionals.

Offer a competitive wage. Peer tutors are selected based on a set of highly specific qualifications, and they receive specialized training in order to accomplish a very high-level set of outcomes. Their wages should reflect this. We all can do only what's possible within our budgets, but strive to offer an hourly wage that honors the high caliber of work that tutors accomplish. Be prepared to articulate to your campus's student employment office why peer tutors merit a spot close to the top of your institution's student employee pay schedule.

Provide tutors with a dependable schedule. Peer tutors should have the benefit of a relatively fixed weekly schedule, so that they know what times will be available for their many other commitments and so that they can count on a paycheck of a certain amount. When the center is slow, tutors should be refocused on special projects for the center (see chapter 5) and on outreach activities (see chapter 5); when the center is busy, tutors should take on additional hours only if they explicitly wish to do so and are able to do so without interfering with their academic commitments. Paying tutors on a "by appointment" basis, offering compensation only for those times when students make appointments with them, is an execrable practice that shows little regard for the value of tutors.

Respect tutors' academic obligations. Student employees are students first and employees second. Students' work as peer tutors should never interfere with their ability to be outstanding students. Adopt policies (in hiring, in granting time off, in schedule flexibility) that respect the time investment involved in being a student and that ensure tutors are able to comfortably maintain the academic behaviors that made them good candidates as tutors in the first place.

Compensate tutors for the time they spend in training. Tutors should always be renumerated for the time they spend engaged in required professional development for the center. Whether it's attending training, doing readings, working on projects, or engaging in peer observations: if it's a mandatory part of employment and doesn't count toward academic credit, employees should be paid for the time they spend doing it.

One way of doing this is by allowing tutors the space to make decisions based on their experience, training, and insight. It's often the case, as professional pedagogues (and, in many cases, as advanced practitioners in the disciplines tutored within the center) that we may observe a situation in which we see a better way for a tutor to handle a scenario with a student. Intervening in the moment undermines the relationship between tutor and learner(s) and deprives tutors of the opportunity to grow as educators by learning from their mistakes. When it is absolutely necessary to inform tutors of serious departures from the norm in applying tutoring pedagogy or in their understanding of the content being tutored, this should be done privately, in a quiet moment after the session has ended. It's absolutely essential to the peer tutoring model that students feel autonomy, power, and trust in their role as tutors.

Another way of creating a positive culture of employment for tutors is by having their backs. Students who aren't yet familiar with the "teach someone to fish" philosophy of peer tutoring may visit the center seeking immediate and straightforward answers to their questions, or for tutors to check over and correct their work (or even, in extreme cases, to do it for them). This can result in frustration, as students encounter tutors' strategies for turning students' questions back on them, for making sure they are the ones doing the work, and for making them active in their own process for learning. Such frustrations can, and often do, materialize in complaints from center users. Often, these results will come not directly, but through faculty who referred students to the center and may themselves be frustrated at hearing a report from their students that the center wasn't helpful.

Every complaint, from every quarter, should be listened to with respect and acted on if necessary. But it's important for you, as an LCA, to realize that many complaints will arise not from anything tutors did wrong, but from tensions between students' expectations and the reality of peer tutoring. Tutors need to know that they have your support. Whenever possible, take advantage of such situations as opportunities to advocate for tutors, educating students and faculty on the pedagogies that drive the choices that tutors make.

Involving tutors, to the greatest extent possible, as decision makers in the center is fundamental to building a center that is a good place for students to work. Feeling a sense of agency, that one's input is valued, and that change is something for us to participate in rather than have inflicted on us, is essential to employees' sense of well-being in any work environment. For learning centers, in which it's critical to attract outstanding students with an aptitude for peer tutoring and to retain them in order to capitalize on the heavy investment on students that we make in tutor training, it's all the more important to create an organization in which student employees experience a sense of agency within the center.

Ways of accomplishing this are many and varied: include tutors' voices on an advisory council. Allow tutors to decorate or organize the center. Provide tutors with a way to provide feedback and have it responded to. Facilitate meetings at which tutors have the opportunity to weigh in on issues that they see emerging in the center and strategize potential solutions. Centers in which tutors have a voice are centers in which tutors experience belonging and engagement, which materializes in every interaction with learners. As an added benefit, centers are far more cued in on and responsive to the needs of students by virtue of having leveraged their student employees as a resource.

Providing avenues for students with ways to explore their interests and accomplish meaningful projects are, likewise, opportunities to simultaneously increase the sense of satisfaction that tutors have in their work and to enrich the center. Having students engage in projects for the center (e.g., creating a workshop, online resource, or poster) or serve as part of a team that collaborates on a larger initiative (e.g., implementing the center's social media presence, maintaining an active newsletter, developing and implementing a tutoring initiative for a new campus location or group) are all ways for students to develop employable skills and begin to build and explore a professional identity. Sending groups of tutors to attend and/or present at regional or national peer tutoring conferences, or involving students in research projects and publications are incredible ways to support students with a strong scholarly interest in the work of peer tutoring in their growth as educators, and to provide students with a record of scholarly activity that will prove a profound asset in future applications for graduate programs. Creating avenues for upward mobility in the center is another way to simultaneously enrich the culture of employment and enrich the center. Positions of leadership within the center create a goal that outstanding tutors can strive toward—providing veteran tutors with ways to gain experience in a leadership role while also amplifying students' voices within the program and sharing the administrative load of overseeing the center.

Finally, and above all else, create a positive culture of employment by expressing gratitude at every opportunity for the hard, good work that peer

STUDENT LEADERSHIP ROLES WITHIN THE CENTER

Many centers offer leadership positions for students who have accrued significant experience as peer tutors and have displayed a particular degree of conscientiousness, leadership ability, and/or acumen in working with students. Often referred to as lead tutors or student managers, these students have responsibilities beyond those of other tutors that may include:

- Modeling excellence in peer-led learning
- Leading, or assisting in leading, trainings or check-in meetings for groups of peer tutors
- Leading or coordinating a team (e.g., writing tutors, SI leaders, chemistry tutors) of peer tutors
- Serving as a liaison to academic departments or to partner programs
- Assisting with the administrative work of the center (e.g., managing the appointment scheduling system, creating advertising materials, maintaining a social media presence)

For tutors demonstrating a particular interest and enthusiasm for learning center work, leadership roles provide an opportunity to participate more fully in the work of the center, gain a highly employable set of professional skills, demonstrate a record of increasing responsibilities, and be closely mentored as leaders and as educators.

tutors accomplish for the center. Excellent tutoring is cognitively (and, often, emotionally) taxing work, and the commitment to work on behalf of their fellow students while still working to honor their own obligations as students is incredibly admirable. End-of-term celebrations, passing along kudos from faculty and administrators, tutor-of-the-week posts on social media, sharing positive feedback from learners, and simply taking note, on an individual basis, of excellent work observed in the center are all simple ways to demonstrate the appreciation that you and others have for the work that peer tutors do. National Tutor Appreciation Week, celebrated in the first full week of October in college learning and writing centers across the country, is an ideal opportunity to organize activities that show tutors how important and valued their work is. Peer tutoring makes the institution a better place and makes a real difference in students' lives. It deserves to be honored at every opportunity.

MODELS FOR INVOLVING STUDENTS IN THE CENTER

In 2019, Julia Bleakney reported a series of in-depth interviews with administrators at nine college writing centers (following up on a larger survey in which 154 institutions participated) with tutor training programs that go beyond a session at the beginning of employment, lasting throughout a tutor's tenure in the center. As one component of the interview, Bleakney asked center directors about techniques that they used to motivate tutors to deeper involvement in the center, beyond the work of engaging with learners. The interviews revealed the following practices for developing tutors as leaders and involving them in center administration (paras. 20–21):

- "tutors serving on committees to plan aspects of the center's work or running the day-to-day operations"
- "tutors having a great deal of autonomy and authority"
- "tutors hav[ing] full control over the weekly meetings"
- "tutors getting more deeply involved by running activities, leading discussions to share their disciplinary expertise, and writing modules for CRLA [trainings] or handouts for center use"
- "ask[ing] . . . experienced tutors to mentor new ones"
- "The director runs a 'leadership institute,' which brings new leadership staff together with existing leaders to 'talk about the challenges they've had and how they dealt with them.'"
- "focus on tutors as members of a professional organization"

Practices such as these strengthen tutors' investment in the center by involving them in ways that build on their developing expertise. They support the educational benefit of tutoring by encouraging tutors to apply concepts in new ways. And they support tutors' development as leaders and professionals, helping them to develop skills that will transfer to the workforce.

RULES AND POLICIES FOR STUDENT EMPLOYMENT

Rules and policies provide a basic structure that everyone involved with the center can depend on. It's simply not possible for a program as operationally complex as a learning center to function without standards that everyone within the center (LCAs and tutors alike) can count on and that guarantee quality and consistency for the students who use the center.

Rules themselves aren't the point. More important than policies, ultimately, are the reasons underlying them. Centers with a positive culture of employment don't simply state rules and hold employees to them; they advance values that provide a rationale for shared standards of behavior (e.g., tutors shouldn't show up late for shifts—not simply because doing so would violate a rule, but because it breaks the promises that the center makes to learners, through its advertising, of when services will be available to learners, and it places an unfair burden on their coworkers). However, part of creating a positive culture of employment is establishing standards that provide a structure to succeed within and hold tutors accountable to one another and to the students who use the center. A position as a peer tutor is a rare opportunity for students to gain professional experience within their field, and part of this acculturation is learning to operate within professional standards for employment.

RULES FOR STUDENT EMPLOYEES

Based on our experiences, these are the rules that we would suggest considering. Rules for employment should be a part of new employee training, and a set of rules and policies should be made available for reference in a printed or online resource.

- No headphones or earbuds may be worn while on shift.
- Phones should be stowed away if not being used for work purposes (e.g., checking for an e-mail from a professor) or as a part of a learning interaction (e.g., accessing an online resource).
- Name tags (or other visual identification of tutors) must be worn at all times while on shift.
- Tutors must be on time for and present in the center for the full duration of all scheduled shifts.
- All absences from scheduled shifts must be cleared in advance with a supervisor, making every effort to find a replacement.
- If tutors need to step away from their scheduled work time for an acceptable reason, they need to notify a supervisor or colleague.
- All scheduled tutor trainings are mandatory.

- Tutors are responsible for all information sent out through e-mail (or other official channels).
- Tutors must not reveal information on a student's academic performance or use of the center to anyone not expressly authorized to have such information.
- Tutors may attend to their own academic work only after first, helping all learners actively seeking support; second, proactively approaching learners who may need support but have not asked; and, finally, attending to other work for the center.

In addition to rules, centers should have clearly delineated policies regarding what happens when they are violated. These are important to have in place so that in situations in which the values that drive the work of the center are not being upheld, a straightforward, transparent, and universally applied set of policies determines what action will be taken (e.g., what scenarios may result in a face-to-face conversation with a supervisor, not being invited back as a tutor in subsequent semesters, or immediate dismissal). One common tool for creating accountability and transparency is the use of an employment contract that tutors sign at the beginning of their employment (or each term in which they are employed) that explicitly states the center's standards for employment and spells out the consequences—up through the invalidation of the contract—for not following them.

In holding peer tutors to standards for employment, always remember that peer tutors are students first and employees second: they are balancing their work as tutors with an enormous set of academic obligations, and they deserve our understanding and support when these come into tension with one another and with the many demands placed on college students' time and attention. This must be weighed against the concern that it's simply not acceptable for learners to have negative experiences in the center as a result of standards of employment not being upheld. The experience that learners have when they access the center is incredibly important to the outcomes of that session, both in terms of learning and of students' likelihood to return. Further, stories of late, unwelcoming, or unhelpful tutors spread quickly, affecting the center's reputation. It's important to maintain the overall quality of services, which means making sure that standards for employment are upheld. This can and should be done with compassion, respect, and empathy, but it must be done.

Peer tutors who are satisfied as employees of the center—who feel included, who perceive that they have a voice within the center, who see

PERFORMANCE REVIEWS

Frequent and specific feedback on performance is one of the keys to student employment functioning effectively as a high-impact practice (Kuh et al., 2005; McClellan, Creager, & Savoca, 2018). In order to grow and develop as peer educators and as professionals, it's important for tutors to have the benefit of timely, constructive feedback focused on helping them improve. Regularly occurring (e.g., once/term) individual performance reviews provide the opportunity to recognize good work, pointing out areas in which peer tutors are exemplifying the values of the center (e.g., making students feel welcome in the center, encouraging active learning, being proactive as a liaison with academic units). They are also an opportunity to address any issues that may have emerged with respect either to their tutoring practice (e.g., providing answers to students questions rather than helping them to find answers themselves, failing to make use of techniques for fostering collaborative learning in a group venue, demonstrating a lack of willingness to try approaches outside their comfort zone), or alignment with the center's guidelines for employment (e.g., being on time for shifts, participating in trainings, seeking advance notice for time off). Feedback should be formative, providing tutors with a clear idea of what specific changes in behavior are being asked of them.

Regular performance reviews also provide an opportunity to check in with tutors, discussing their goals, their lives as students, and challenges they may be facing in applying their training to their work with learners. Potential sources of information to inform performance reviews include peer observations, patterns in student feedback, and observed behaviors, as well as records such as time clock data and sign-ins for tutor trainings.

Of course, it's not necessary to wait for performance reviews to offer feedback. Noticing and commenting on tutoring excellence in the moment is a powerful way to make tutors feel appreciated. Serious issues that could affect students' experience of using the center should always be addressed quickly. Performance reviews have a more holistic role, providing tutors with clear direction on the path forward in their development.

meaning in the work they do, who have a clear sense of the structure within which they operate, and who view the center as a venue for growth and development—are peer tutors who bring their best selves to their work. Happy, motivated tutors are the most essential ingredient of a well-functioning, mission-oriented center. All other aspects of learning center administration are secondary to hiring great students and creating a culture that will inspire them to accomplish outstanding work.

QUESTIONS FOR PROGRAM ASSESSMENT

Hiring

- Does the center's hiring process ensure (generally through faculty references, but potentially through other mechanisms) that students have sufficient command of the material they will be tutoring to provide meaningful guidance for learners?
- Does the hiring process ensure that students who are hired as tutors understand what it is to struggle as a learner and are able to demonstrate empathy for learners who are having difficulty in a course?
- Does the hiring process provide (generally through interviews, but potentially through other mechanisms) significant weight to nonacademic factors such as communication skills, interpersonal warmth, a capacity for growth, and a willingness to face uncomfortable situations?
- Does the hiring process result in a team of tutors that collectively are able to support a wide variety of student needs?
- Does the hiring process result in a team of tutors that mirrors the diversity that exists on campus, representing (if possible, overrepresenting) minority students on the center staff?
- Is the hiring process spaced out throughout the year in a way that is transparent for students and makes the work of hiring sustainable for the center's LCA(s)?
- Does the hiring process invite participation and investment from students, staff, and faculty stakeholders?

Culture of Student Employment

- Do the tutors have autonomy, trusted in most situations to work with learners without direct supervision or interference?
- Do the tutors know that in instances when implementing the pedagogies they are training on (e.g., redirecting questions back to learners) results in tensions with learners or with faculty, they will have the support of the LCA(s)?
- Do tutors experience agency within the center, allowed opportunities to participate as decision makers in significant aspects of its administration?
- Do tutors have opportunities to explore areas of personal interest and develop employable professional skills that align with their career goals?
- Do tutors have opportunities for advancement to positions of greater responsibility and leadership within the center?
- Do tutors experience being valued for the important work they do for the center and the important role that they fulfill on campus?

Rules and Policies for Student Employment

- Does the center have a clear set of rules and standards for employment that are made clear to tutors in their initial training and are always available in a printed or online format?
- Does the center have clear guidelines for what happens in scenarios where standards for employment are not followed, and are these guidelines made clear to tutors in their initial training and always available in a printed or online format?
- Do these rules guarantee the smooth operation of the center and a high standard of services for learners?
- Do these rules and guidelines have sufficient flexibility to honor the fact that peer tutors are successful students and that their employment should offer sufficient flexibility for them to remain so?

Chapter Five

Tutor Training

Peer tutors, in their work with students, bring learners into collaboration with one another. They involve students as active participants in learning and, in the process, support them in approaching all educational venues as active learners. They support learners in developing toward mastery by providing scaffolding that allows learners to operate at the edges of their knowledge and abilities. They help students develop a critical awareness of their own processes for learning, as well as strategies and habits that will empower them as successful learners. And they attend to students as unique learners, tailoring their approaches to individuals mindful of the diverse identities that students being to the center and to students' current point in their journey as learners. These are all complex pedagogies, dependent on tutors' abilities to respond quickly and capably, in the moment, to draw out information from learners and use that information to drive choices on how to implement the most effective support. A fundamental aspect of supporting tutors in their work with learners is implementing a training program that provides tutors with the theoretical and practical knowledge to foster academic success in their peers and promotes tutors' continuing growth as educators.

THE EFFECT OF TRAINING ON STRATEGIES FOR TUTORING

Robust tutor training is a defining feature of learning centers and a major contributing factor to the impact that learning centers have on students. In the absence of training, students' preconceptions about tutoring and the type of approach they find most natural based on their innate tendencies are the most powerful predictors of the tools that they use in working with learners

(Berghmans et al., 2013; Velasco & Stains, 2015). An effective peer tutor training program counters these tutor-oriented factors with learner-oriented strategies, steering tutors toward approaches that may initially feel less comfortable
or intuitive but are, in fact, more effective for students using peer tutoring.

Building on earlier research indicating that tutor training is a critical component in the effectiveness of tutoring programs (Boylan et al., 1997; Fantuzzo
et al., 1989) and that tutor training has a real, measurable effect on the strategies that tutors use in sessions with learners (Chadwick & McGuire, 2004;
Cromley & Azevedo, 2005; Graesser et al., 1995; Schleyer et al., 2005), Bailey
(2010) reported the results of an observational study that compared tutoring
interactions involving trained tutors in a learning center with untrained tutors
in a departmental tutoring program. He found that untrained tutors used less-
effective tutoring strategies than their trained counterparts in learning centers—
using less relational communication, making fewer efforts to assess learners'
comprehension, relying more heavily on explanations, failing to direct learners
toward higher-level thinking, making more limited use of active learning strategies and academic skills, and employing a smaller set of helping strategies.

GOALS FOR TUTOR TRAINING

A common misconception about tutor training among students, faculty, and
administrators is that training for tutors consists of teaching or reviewing
content that tutors will, in turn, relay to learners. Were this the case, tutor
training would have a function that overlaps almost completely with students'
courses. In learning centers, we hire students who, while still learners themselves, have developed both the cognitive (e.g., ideas, processes, skills) and
metacognitive (e.g., strategies, academic habits, study skills) knowledge to
succeed within a curriculum. The training that we provide empowers tutors
to leverage that knowledge to help other students succeed as well.

Provide Tutors with the Skills and Knowledge They Will Need

This means appreciating the goals and context of their work with students,
especially the peer tutoring model and the role of learning centers within
institutions of higher education. It means understanding how learning works,
to center their work supporting students as learners. It means imparting tools
and strategies that are demonstrably effective for supporting the growth of
college students as learners, thinkers, and writers. And it means supporting
peer tutors in responding to the students they work with as individual learners, through an appreciation of all the ways in which students vary. An effective peer tutor training program empowers tutors to make effective, informed
choices in their work with students, drawing on a solid understanding of how
learning works, of pedagogy, and of the underpinnings of academic success.

TOPICS FOR TUTOR TRAINING

It's beyond the scope of this text to engage in-depth with specific tutor training topics, but a list is provided below of topics in tutor training that together represent a full curriculum that provides tutors with support in making informed choices in the work that they do with learners. The topics below are explored fully in *The Rowman & Littlefield Guide for Peer Tutors* (Sanford, 2020). It provides an in-depth treatment for each of the topics provided here for peer tutors and a suggested training structure learning center administrators can use in delivering both individual trainings and an overall curriculum.

Introduction to Peer Tutoring. The peer tutoring model, the benefits of peer tutoring for learners and for tutors, the history and mission of learning centers, students' right to privacy (and peer tutors' role in enforcing legislation related to it).

Learning and the Brain. Cognitive schemas, working memory and long-term memory, cognitive load theory, metaphor and analogy, metacognition.

Pedagogy. Constructivism, active learning, collaborative learning, the zone of proximal development, scaffolding, diagnostic questions.

Working with Students. The major formats for peer tutoring, techniques for time management, strategies for facilitating learning interactions between students in groups, appropriately referring students among tutoring formats.

The Affective Domain. Peer tutoring as coaching, the way that students' emotional and physiological states affect their ability to learn, embodied cognition, Bloom's taxonomy (the affective domain), active listening, motivation, belonging.

Learning Strategies. First-year students, research-based strategies for time management, note taking, reading and writing papers, modeling learning strategies, identifying situations in which learning strategies should be a focus.

Engaging a Diverse Student Body. The role that learning centers play in supporting diversity, strategies for engaging with students across racial diversity, cultural diversity, linguistic diversity and neurodiversity, universal design for learning, antiracism, allyship, implicit bias.

Fostering Critical Thinking. Critical thinking, Bloom's Taxonomy (the cognitive domain), discipline-specific ways of knowing, writing, thinking, and problem solving, cognitive biases, discipline-specific metacognitive strategies.

Peer Tutoring in Online Environments. How the peer tutoring model unfolds in online environments, the major formats of online tutoring, asynchronous and synchronous tutoring, theories of online communication, theories of online learning.

Other Ways to Engage as a Tutor. Liaising with academic departments, special projects for the center (e.g., handouts, workshops, online tutorials, tutor trainings), peer observations, academic engagement (academic conferences, publications), leadership within the center, statements of peer educator philosophy.

Allow Students to Practice Skills They Will Need

As essential as understanding the ideas and concepts that underlie tutoring is for learners, being able to fluently deploy that knowledge within a learning scenario means developing practical, hands-on strategies for doing so and becoming versed in using them. It's one thing, for example, to understand that learning strategies are important. It's another thing entirely to be comfortable and confident in redirecting a session toward an underlying issue with note taking, time management, or studying (or to be comfortable and confident in asking the diagnostic questions that would allow a tutor to understand when such a turn may be called for). It's not enough for tutors to have a theoretical understanding of their work, or even to have carefully thought through what they plan to do in sessions. Working with a student to negotiate a plan for a session, redirecting questions back toward learners, placing students in small groups to compare notes, facilitating a collaborative activity, directing a student toward a different format of tutoring, putting a paper/piece of homework back in front of a student to keep him active in the learning process, wrapping up a session: these and many other aspects of peer tutoring are skills that take time to master. For inexperienced tutors, they can be not only intimidating but barriers to implementing effective pedagogy.

Tutor training should provide an opportunity for tutors to try out, in a low-stakes and supportive venue, the moves that successful tutors make in tutoring sessions with learners. Formats of tutoring, similarly, should be trained in a practical and hands-on sense, with tutors having the opportunity to practice not only formats of tutoring that they will be using, but also formats others use in the center so they can develop a deep appreciation for all of the services offered within the center (and, therefore, are able to refer students to other those other services based on a deep, thorough understanding of how they work and what they entail).

IDEAS FOR TUTOR TRAININGS

Varying the format of tutors' trainings is an important part of keeping them interesting and engaging for tutors. This list provides a few possibilities.

- Discuss challenging scenarios that came up in the learning center that week.
- Provide a 10-minute overview of a topic from the science of learning; allow tutors to explore in small-group discussions the relevance of the topic to their work in the center.
- Have tutors generate prompts that set up challenging tutoring situations and write them on a piece of paper, then have tutors randomly select them and act them out in pairs or small groups.

- Have tutors develop and act out tutoring scenarios that demonstrate the applications of specific ideas from a recent training.
- Have tutors work in pairs or groups to practice specific tutoring strategies (e.g., asking diagnostic questions), taking turns playing the role of tutor and learner.
- Invite a guest trainer from a partner program to speak to the unique needs of specific groups of students (e.g., student athletes, former military students, first-generation college students).
- Devote a training to discussing peer observations that tutors have recently completed.
- Have tutors present (formally, with adequate time for preparation, or informally, with participants generating ideas during the session) on pedagogies/research tools from the academic disciplines they are studying, exploring their relevance to peer tutoring.
- Give each tutor a piece of sticky easel paper to write a tutoring situation they've encountered thus far on which they'd like input; stick them around the room and have all tutors do a "gallery walk" writing helpful tips on everyone's sheet (based on what they've learned in training thus far as well as their own experiences). Ask each tutor to review the tips on her sheets and share one that most resonates with them in terms of handling the situation.
- Have tutors work together within a Google document to use what they've learned to develop a tutor evaluation rubric that they feel encapsulates the most important components in any good tutoring session; let them test it by observing each other using the rubric. Discuss findings at a subsequent training.
- Have tutors interview veteran tutors on ethical issues they've encountered and how they handled them. Have interviewers report out, discussing alternative ways to handle each issue.

Provide Students with the Opportunity for Reflection

A reflective component in tutor training supports tutors in growing from their experiences by providing, whether through writing (Gentle et al., 2015; Zacharopoulou, Giles, & Condell, 2015) or through dialogue with others (Bleakney, 2016; Bunting, 2014), the time and space for tutors to connect the ideas, skills, and concepts that they encounter in training to their tutoring practice. Reflection can guide tutors toward using new aspects of learning-center theory encountered in training as critical lenses for their own work with learners and consideration of the ways that their practice could be improved, helping them to formulate goals for their future interactions with learners. It fosters tutors' professional development, both their development as educators and their ability to speak to that development.

A regular space in training for tutors to speak, think, and write about their shared work with students provides a forum for mentoring, in which less-experienced tutors can gain from the knowledge and insights of more-experienced tutors. What did I learn today? What recent session would I have approached differently if I had had this information? How have I grown as a tutor since I first began this work? What are my intentions for applying these new tools to my future work with students? Devoting time for tutors to reflect on questions such as these allows tutors to develop a sense of their own journey as peer educators, empowering further growth and fostering tutors' sense of their emerging identity as educators and as professionals.

PEER OBSERVATIONS

In peer observations, tutors observe one another in sessions with learners, providing feedback and considering implications for their own work with learners. Often, observations are reciprocal, with tutors either at a similar level of experience (if the goal is mutual development) or different levels of experience (if the goal is for novice tutors to learn from veteran tutors). Peer observations are an outstanding way to assess the impact of trainings, determining whether tools and strategies from trainings are being implemented in actual tutoring interactions in the center. For tutors being observed, peer feedback can provide valuable information that they can use to improve their own work with learners. Peer observation provides perhaps the most critical benefit for the tutors who are doing the observing, as it allows them the opportunity to see approaches other than their own, to consider the variety of ways that effective tutoring can be implemented, and to incorporate impactful strategies within the set of techniques with which they feel comfortable. Peer observations are an opportunity for reflection, providing tutors with a highly structured way to consider their own work as tutors with guidance from others and in relation to others.

Peer observation, in order to be effective, should be highly specific—tutors should head into peer observations with a clear idea of what specific things they are paying attention to. This guidance can be provided by a form that provides a rubric for peer observation (Sanford, 2020). Peer observation can also follow up on recent trainings, with tutors directed to pay attention to how their observation partners are implementing tools and concepts from a recent training (e.g., how they are engaging in active learning following a training on the affective domain of learning). Following an observation cycle, tutors can exchange observation forms with one another and discuss them in pairs, or an entire meeting can be devoted to a discussion of what was observed in observation sessions.

Crucially, tutors should always seek permission from learners before observing a session, explaining the goals of their observation (and, in particular, that the goal is to assess the tutor, not the learner) and making clear that the learners can and should feel free to decline being observed. As real as the benefits of peer observation are, they are outweighed by students' right to privacy and their overall comfort within the center.

Model the Pedagogies Tutors Will Use

Nothing more effectively undermines trainings for peer tutors than to deliver them in formats modeled on the traditional classroom. Lecturing at peer tutors, or otherwise delivering the content of tutor training in a way that limits the role of tutors to passive recipients of knowledge, sends the clear message that we believe that the very instructor-led, expert-oriented, learning-as-transfer approaches that we advise our tutors to eschew and to which we envision learning centers as alternatives are, in fact, the best way to foster learning. For tutors to have a clear mental model of the pedagogical approaches that the center favors, they need to see them in action.

Tutor trainings are an ideal opportunity to demonstrate practices that follow from active and collaborative approaches to learning, giving tutors the opportunity to try them out from the perspective of a learner while also providing them with templates for tools that they can, in turn, apply in their own work with students. Most powerfully, using learning center pedagogy in our trainings allows us to leverage the benefits of active, collaborative, and learner-led approaches, scaffolding the development of robust knowledge structures for pedagogical approaches. Tutor trainings should look, to a casual observer, very much like a learning center in full swing: busy, active, and vibrant. Tutors should have the opportunity to think through how new ideas relate to their own experiences, to engage deeply with concepts by applying them in realistic scenarios, to work in small groups in which differing points of view can come into contact with one another, and to be part of a learning community in which individuals at different levels of attainment work toward the shared goals of becoming more effective peer educators.

PROS AND CONS OF TRAINING IN COURSE VERSUS PAID TRAININGS

A perennial question in learning centers is whether it's more effective to implement tutor training through paid trainings (incentivizing participation through pay and making it a requirement for employment) or through a course (incentivizing participation through academic credit and making it a pre- or corequisite for employment).

This question has no one right answer, and the optimal solution for each program (whether paid trainings, a tutor training course, or a hybrid of the two) will depend largely on local context. Generally, the advantage of paid tutor trainings is that they are relatively straightforward to implement; and because they are part of student employment, it is easy to create policies around them relating to attendance (and the consequences of nonattendance). Paid trainings are also not bound by the structures of the academic calendar—they can meet before or after the term begins, meet intermittently, or span multiple terms—which makes them well-suited to providing training at whatever point in a tutor's development it is needed.

The major advantages of delivering tutor training in a class is that the structure of a course allows for a deeper, more sustained inquiry into the theory and practice of tutoring than is easily accommodated within paid trainings. In addition, the academic setting of a tutor training course can work very effectively to create a tone of intellectual inquiry that can be harder (although by no means impossible) to establish within paid trainings. In addition, tutor training courses create a transcripted credential for students that speaks to their training in pedagogy.

Other factors that should be considered are the costs to the center for paying tutors to attend trainings versus the cost of paying (should it be a cost that falls to the center) for an instructor to teach a course, and the relative difficulty of implementing a course within the local academic infrastructure. Especially for centers and LCAs that do not have an affiliation with an academic department, it can be challenging to get a tutor training course cataloged, find a credit-bearing department to host it, and accommodate a teaching obligation within LCA employment contracts.

Be Intellectually Engaging

In hiring peer tutors, we assemble some of the brightest, most motivated, driven, articulate, and insightful students on campus, and we place them in an educational space together with the expectation that they're there to learn. What we do in that space has to honor that premise.

Tutor trainings should challenge tutors with unfamiliar, engaging ideas, pushing them forward in their growth as educators by placing them at the edge of their knowledge and abilities, beyond their comfort zones. Training should challenge tutors' preconceptions about the mind, learning, diversity, student success, and other aspects of peer tutoring, forcing tutors to grow as pedagogues by presenting them with ideas and concepts that can't be accommodated within their existing knowledge structures. Tutor trainings should encourage them to draw connections between the ideas they are being exposed to as tutors and the concepts they are studying as students, inviting them to explore the relevance of ideas from the disciplines they are studying—methods, theoretical lenses, problem-solving approaches, disciplinary modes of thinking—to learning center theory and to consider how the tools that peer tutors use apply to the unique issues that learners encounter within their own areas of study. Tutor trainings should invite tutors to participate within the exciting, emerging field of learning center theory and the broader scholarship of higher education teaching and learning, exposing them directly to the new theoretical approaches and new findings on the cognition of learning that are constantly coming into being.

Finally, trainings should challenge tutors to reach to find the implications of new ideas for their tutoring practices themselves, rather than presenting them as lists of "dos" and "don'ts" for tutoring. Students who become tutors do so for many reasons, but one of the most dependable (and the major reason that the students who become tutors are so wonderful to work with) is that they are caring individuals who want to help. For smart students, motivated by wanting to do their work as well as possible, it's neither necessary nor beneficial to present learning center theory as a set of rules and precepts. Pedagogy is a domain of inquiry that encompasses a diversity of thought and within which intelligent people can and do disagree. Tutor training should revel in complexity, inviting tutors to active learning in the realm of pedagogy by encouraging them to draw conclusions for themselves rather than thrusting conclusions upon them.

NEUROMYTHS: HEMISPHERE DOMINANCE AND LEARNING STYLES

The term "neuromyth" describes a widespread popular misconception about the brain based on a mistaken, flawed, or simply erroneous understanding of brain research (e.g., the common, false idea that humans use only 10% of their brains). Coined by neurosurgeon Alan Crockard in 1980, and developed and popularized by a 2002 report of the Organisation for Economic Co-operation and Development that defined neuromyths as "misconception[s] generated by a misunderstanding, a misreading or a misquoting of facts scientifically established (by brain research) to make a case for use of brain research, in education and other contexts" (p. 111), the term labels a highly common phenomenon. Neuromyths have incredible persistence, perpetuated in society and even within academic disciplines despite having no basis in fact. Two neuromyths in particular are pervasive within learning center theory, commonly found in tutor trainings despite having no acceptance within learning science.

Hemisphere dominance is the idea that the left hemisphere of the brain is more numerical and logical while the right hemisphere of the brain is more creative and visual, that individuals are more dominant in their right or left hemispheres (e.g., an artistic individual might be referred to as "right-brained"), and that educators should tailor instruction accordingly. These ideas are based on an outdated view of the brain and misunderstood research findings. Although some brain functions are lateralized, all higher cognitive functions involve both sides of the brain (Herve et al., 2013; Tzourio-Mazoyer, Crivello, & Mazoyer, 2017; Wagner et al., 2003). In a 2013 study analyzing MRIs from more than a thousand individuals, Nielsen et al. found no significant variation regarding right versus left dominance in the strength of neural networks across individuals.

Learning styles is the idea that individuals fall into categories generally aligning with the senses according to how they think and learn: visual, auditory, or kinesthetic (with other categories included as well in some schemes); and that as educators we can help individuals to learn effectively by tailoring instruction for individual students according to their learning styles—not to be confused with Howard Gardner's (2006) influential theory of multiple intelligences, which Gardner himself has taken pains to distance from the idea of learning styles (Strauss, 2013). Pashler et al. (2008), in a comprehensive review of the extant available empirical research on learning styles, found no credible evidence to support the hypothesis that taking learning styles into account has an instructional benefit, asserting, "The contrast between the enormous popularity of the learning-styles approach within education and the lack of credible evidence for its utility is . . . striking and disturbing" (p. 117).

Although we have many beneficial ways to attend to students as individual learners, hemisphere dominance and learning styles are not valid ways to do so. They are demonstrably false ideas that have long been discredited and have no place in any tutor training curriculum that purports to be grounded in research principles.

Allow Tutors to Engage with Other Tutors and Break into Teams

A general grounding in peer tutoring is relevant to all tutors, and it has a very important benefit (closely tied to the nature of a learning center as a program that centralizes peer tutoring) to all tutors within a center training together so that they develop relationships across teams, an appreciation for the work that tutors do in other areas, and a sense of cohort.

It's also important, however, that tutors have opportunities to separate by disciplinary area (e.g., chemistry tutors, humanities tutors) and/or by the general format of tutoring that they work within (e.g., workshop leaders, drop-in lab tutors). Breakout trainings allow tutors to compare notes with their closest peers in the center, engaging over shared challenges and reflecting on the types of recurring situations that tutors who work in similar roles encounter in their interactions with learners (team training is a particularly good format for trainings dedicated to decompressing recent tutoring sessions, talking through particularly interesting or challenging sessions, and discussing the lessons that emerged from them). They can provide a space for tutors to discuss the ways that more general principles in peer tutoring play out within the specific kinds of tutoring interaction that take place within the disciplines that they support.

They create a space for teams of tutors associated with strongly developed fields of practice within the more general field of peer tutoring (e.g., writing center tutors, SI/PASS leaders) to dive into the scholarship associated with those fields of practice. They supply a forum for groups of tutors who are directly familiar with the challenges of a specific curriculum (e.g., lower-division courses for a physics major) to strategize providing support for learners who are navigating that same curriculum, considering common stumbling blocks (e.g., vectors), and working together to develop approaches for helping learners overcome them. And they allow tutors to consider signature pedagogies—the particular ways that teaching takes place within individual academic disciplines, reflecting the specific values and habits of mind cultivated within areas of study that prepare students to serve as thinkers, writers, academics, and practitioners in their fields (Chick et al., 2009; Schulman, 2005)—thinking through how they can support learners who are navigating the unique challenges associated with that pedagogy. Groups of tutors who have developed an awareness of signature pedagogies within their own fields can, in turn, consider how these approaches might be helpful to learners in other areas as well. A good balance of center-wide tutor trainings and breakout trainings by team provides not only a space for teams to cultivate expertise in approaches that are particularly well-suited to the subjects they tutor and the formats for tutoring they work within but also a forum for these ideas to flow between individual teams and to enrich the center as a whole.

CRLA INTERNATIONAL TUTOR TRAINING PROGRAM CERTIFICATION

The International Tutor Training Program administered by the College Reading and Learning Association ("International Tutor Training Program Certification [ITTPC]," 2018) is a popular system for certifying college tutor training programs. Learning centers submit applications that are vetted through CRLA to certify at levels I (Regular), II (Advanced), or III (Master). CRLA training certification at each level mandates a number of training topics from a list of topics and completion of a set number of hours engaged in peer tutoring interactions.

CRLA tutor training offers a number of advantages for participating centers. The cachet of certification is one factor to consider. The widespread adoption of CRLA training standards has resulted in certification filling the role of a basic standard of maturity for learning centers, indicating that a center operates within the parameters of a broadly accepted set of best practices for hiring and training peer tutors. CRLA certification also serves as an indicator, for local stakeholders, that the center has attained a degree of national recognition, and adheres to a set of recognized standards (messaging that can and should be advanced through campus media for centers that have adopted CRLA certification). It makes it simple to articulate, by pointing toward CRLA standards, the comprehensive training that peer educators undergo. For tutors, CRLA certification through the center provides a clear credential that they can use in subsequent applications for employment to speak to their training and experience as a peer tutor. Most important, CRLA tutor training certification imposes a degree of consistency in tutor training. A CRLA-certified program can be argued to have fully covered its bases in ensuring that tutors have the basic training they need to excel as tutors, and the process of preparing and applying for certification is one good way to develop a clear, organized structure for tutor training. The standards, outcomes, and assessment measures that ITTPC suggests provide a clear path, especially for new centers, toward a training curriculum that offers peer tutors robust guidance and support.

CRLA's system of certification also has significant limitations. It tends to assume one-to-one forms of tutoring (most seriously, CRLA certification explicitly excludes from its purview SI/PASS (see chapter 4), a highly widespread form of peer tutoring that is within the suite of services offered by many learning centers. It involves a very significant recurring cost (both financially and in terms of the labor involved in tracking tutor advancement, certification, and cyclical recertification [see also Devet, 2006]) that may be particularly onerous for smaller and/or less robustly staffed programs. Finally, as a standardizing program, ITTPC is by nature conservative. CRLA certification provide the flexibility for centers to explore recent scholarship that is not explicitly indicated in ITTPC outcomes, such as cognition-based strategies that are highly effective in aiding learning (e.g., distributed practice [Benjamin & Tullis, 2010; Cepeda et al., 2006; Janiszewski, Noel, & Sawyer, 2003], repeated recall [Krug, Davis, & Glover, 1990; McDaniel & Masson, 1985; Smith et al., 2016] or interleaving [Carpenter & Mueller, 2013; Richland et al., 2005; Rohrer, 2012; Rohrer, Dedrick, & Stershic, 2015]) or the rapid development that has taken place in writing center theory over the past two decades in particular in theorizing how centers for peer tutoring can engage with complex issues of diversity, equity, and social justice. However, it tends to steer trainers toward older, more established aspects of learning center scholarship over emerging topics such as these. Notably, a round of 2021 updates has done much to modernize and improve ITTPC guidelines.

Whether these weaknesses outweigh the benefits of ITTPC certification is a question each center should determine based on local needs. One possible middle ground is a locally created tutor certification offering a clear structure for tutor training, drawing from elements of ITTPC but more suited to the needs of an individual center. Such a certification can provide learning centers with a clear message to campus stakeholders regarding the thorough training provided for tutors, and to tutors regarding the professional development they received through their work with the center, while also being ideally more reflective than ITTPC of recent trends in scholarship.

Accommodate Tutors' Growth over Time

A comprehensive training program should consider not only new tutors, but also those who are returning to employment as peer tutors over the course of successive years: how will their growing experience and expertise as peer educators, as well as their growth and development in their own studies, be accommodated? Those who are returning for successive terms as tutors should be provided with new ways to engage with the ideas presented in trainings, exploring progressively more advanced ideas in pedagogy (e.g., through discussion of a reading on an emerging area of pedagogy, or sharing informal research projects on aspects of learning center theory that aren't touched on in introductory trainings).

One common way for centers to leverage the experience and expertise of returning tutors while also pushing them forward in their growth as educators is by recruiting them to create projects for the center (handouts, online tutorials, posters, study guides, etc.) grounded in the pedagogical principles about which they've learned. Another is by recruiting experienced tutors as trainers, facilitating (or helping to facilitate) trainings in which they mentor less-experienced tutors, providing insight based on their experience while applying their pedagogical training in a new way (and developing a highly desirable professional skill). Experienced tutors can easily become disaffected or unengaged if they aren't included in training—or, even worse, if they have to sit through the same sessions term after term. Using returning tutors as resources keeps them engaged and motivated while also empowering the center to benefit from tutors' accumulated experience over time.

Effective, impactful peer tutoring is not necessarily intuitive. Peer tutors are, among many other things, successful students who know the material that they tutor well, have the verbal ability to capably articulate it, and are empathetic individuals drawn to the work of academic support. It's the most natural thing in the world for such a student, asked a question by a peer in need of help, to open his mouth and let the knowledge come out, providing an explanation that fully addresses the learner's question. Such a response, however—although certainly one tool in a tutor's toolkit, and appropriate in some situations—is generally less effective than strategies that invoke learners' existing knowledge, encourage more effective learning strategies, leverage their fellow students as co-learners, and create learners who are aware of resources at their disposal for finding the answers to their questions themselves. An effective tutor training program provides tutors with the knowledge base to understand why such strategies are advantageous and the opportunity to develop ease and fluency in doing so. And at all times, it invites tutors into a deeper understanding of the theory that underlies their work with learners and to participation within the academic communities associated with peer-led learning in higher education.

SAMPLE ANNUAL TRAINING SEQUENCE

The fundamental challenge in implementing a tutor training program is to get tutors the information, theories, strategies, and tools they need, when they need them—tutors should neither be in a position to engage in tutoring sessions without adequate training, nor to receive extensive training without having had sufficient experience to be able to understand the relevance of the concepts they are being exposed to. A well-designed tutor training curriculum should provide tutors with enough information up front to adequately prepare them to work with students; as time goes on, the curriculum introduces new ideas while allowing tutors to accrue enough experience to perceive their relevance and then to implement them accordingly. This schedule provides one of many possible ways of distributing training topics throughout a year, assuming the most typical two-semester system.

Tutor trainings for tutors returning for 3+ semesters might focus on special projects or readings on advanced topics, or involve tutors as trainers in the first-year curriculum.

	Fall Semester	**Spring Semester**
Pre-semester Training	Rules and standards for employment, the mission of the center, learning and the brain, peer tutoring as a pedagogical model, the formats of tutoring used by the center	Checking in, after a semester of tutoring, on the fundamental principles of peer tutoring
Week 1	Team training (check-in, team building)	Team training (check-in, team building)
Week 2	The Affective Domain	Active listening
Week 3	Team training to check in, explore previous week's training by academic discipline and/or tutoring format	Team training to check in, explore previous week's training by academic discipline and/or tutoring format
Week 4	Learning Strategies: Time Management	Learning Strategies: Studying and Note Taking
Week 5	Team training to check in, explore previous week's training by academic discipline and/or tutoring format	Team training to check in, explore previous week's training by academic discipline and/or tutoring format

	Fall Semester	**Spring Semester**
Week 6	Engaging a Diverse Student Body: Racial and Cultural Diversity	Engaging a Diverse Student Body: Neurodiversity
Week 7	Team training to check in, explore previous week's training by academic discipline and/or tutoring format	Team training to check in, explore previous week's training by academic discipline and/or tutoring format
Week 8	Week off to focus on midterms	Week off to focus on midterms
Week 9	Engaging a Diverse Student Body: Linguistic Diversity	Setting up peer observation cycle
Week 10	Team training to check in, explore previous week's training by academic discipline and/or tutoring format	Team training to discuss peer observations
Week 11	Fostering Critical Thinking: Bloom's Taxonomy	Fostering Critical Thinking: Disciplinary Modes of Thinking
Week 12	Team training to check in, explore previous week's training by academic discipline and/or tutoring format	Team training to check in, explore previous week's training by academic discipline and/or tutoring format
Week 13	Week off to focus on finals	Week off to focus on finals
Week 14	End-of-term celebration/tutor recognition event	End-of-year celebration/tutor recognition event

QUESTIONS FOR PROGRAM ASSESSMENT

- Do the center's trainings provide tutors with an understanding of the peer tutoring model and of the role of the learning center on campus?
- Do the trainings provide tutors with an appreciation for the physical processes that underlie learning in the brain and how to take advantage of the brain's cognitive architecture in fostering learning?
- Do the trainings provide tutors with an understanding of the core pedagogies of peer tutoring, especially active and collaborative learning, and of how to apply them in tutoring sessions?

- Do the trainings provide tutors with an in-depth understanding of all of the types and formats of tutoring that are provided within the center (not only those that they themselves provide)?
- Do the trainings provide tutors with an appreciation of the ways that students' emotional states affect their capacity to learn and strategies for attending to learners' emotional states?
- Do the trainings provide tutors with an understanding of effective learning strategies (e.g., note taking, time management, studying, writing papers) that they can use to guide students toward effective academic habits?
- Do the trainings provide tutors with an appreciation for diversity and an understanding of how to be both cognizant and supportive of difference in tutoring scenarios?
- Do the trainings provide tutors with an understanding of strategies for pushing learning toward deeper, more critical thinking (and, in particular, toward disciplinary modes of critical thinking)?
- If the center offers online support, do the centers' trainings provide tutors with an appreciation for the forms of online tutoring and the way that peer tutoring pedagogy plays out within them?
- Do the trainings provide advanced tutors with guidance on deeper engagement with the center, with peer tutoring pedagogy, and/or with learning center theory?
- Do the trainings provide students with opportunities to practice the skills they are learning, allowing them to become comfortable with them before applying them with learners?
- Do the trainings provide tutors with opportunities to reflect on their own growth as educators and on how they will implement the principles and strategies they are learning in training in their future sessions with learners?
- Do the trainings model the pedagogical approaches that tutors are expected to apply in the center, taking advantage of active, collaborative, learner-led approaches?
- Are the trainings challenging for tutors, leveraging tutors' identities as strong students and fostering intellectual engagement with the material being delivered?
- Do the trainings provide tutors with opportunities to meet together with all of the tutors in the center, learning about general principles while developing a sense of shared identity?
- Do the trainings provide tutors with opportunities to meet as teams by discipline and/or format of tutoring, allowing them to consider concerns and issues unique to their group while developing a sense of themselves as specialists?

- Do the trainings support returning tutors in their ongoing growth as peer educators, continually challenging them with new concepts and meaningfully incorporating their experience and expertise?
- Are the trainings structured in a way that provides tutors with the information they need, when they need it? For example, do the center's trainings avoid overwhelming tutors with concepts they don't yet have the context to understand? Do they avoid failing to provide tutors in a timely way with concepts that are essential to their work with learners? Are the trainings spaced out in a way that provide tutors with time to internalize and practice applying a concept before moving on to a new one?

Chapter Six

Designing the Physical Space of the Center

Learning centers are locations for peer-led learning. They are where peer tutoring interactions take place, and one extremely important function that the physical spaces of learning centers provide is supplying the structure and infrastructure to facilitate tutoring. Learning centers are far more, however, than simply spaces for peer tutoring. The physical site of a center realizes the pedagogy that drives it. It is a representation, embodied in design, of the identity and values of the center as an organization. Jamieson (2003, p. 122) asserts that learning environments guide student's experiences by "authorising and enabling certain behaviors over others." The unique learning environment of the learning center authorizes active engagement, collaborative learning, and social interaction, and it enables broad access to higher education through support for diversity. The design of the center must proceed from these considerations.

Moreover, the space of learning centers functions as the most public, widely known aspect of their identity among the stakeholders they serve. As a learning center administrator, you have a robust knowledge of everything that a center comprises and everything that it takes, behind the scenes, to make it function. For most students, tutors, faculty, and administrators, however, the physical space of the center *is* the center. Whether you are considering an entire center or one area within it, whether you are designing a center from the ground up or working to maximize an existing space, and whether your center comprises a dedicated building or a borrowed classroom: you are in a position to make choices that will have a powerful impact on how the space is known and experienced by its users. Its design has to be strong enough to carry that weight and to communicate the identity of the center to everyone who walks through its door.

LOCATION

It's rare for learning program administrators to be able to weigh in on the location for their program. Given the opportunity to do so, it's an incredible chance to affect the way that the center will be perceived. A center in a basement, or in a removed corner of campus, doesn't just miss out on foot traffic. It presents itself as peripheral, outside of the usual day-to-day of campus life. Centers in well-used spaces, particularly in locations that are central to the student experience (libraries, student union buildings, classroom buildings), send the implicit message that accessing peer tutoring is akin to checking out books, grabbing a cup of coffee, or going to class: a normal, regular part of the day-to-day life of a student. The message about its role on campus that the location of the space sends will be heard far more loudly, both by students and by other campus stakeholders, than anything you say as a representative of the program.

Centrality is also a powerful determiner of student usage. Every additional minute of walking time can and will affect the center's utilization figures, which reflect students' collective decisions on whether the benefit that a student hopes to accrue from accessing tutoring outweighs the time and trouble of doing so. It's highly related, as well, to visibility: a center that students see every day is a center in students' conscious awareness, reminding them constantly of the utility that they could receive from it. Larger, less in-demand spaces are commonly found on the edges and quiet corners of campus and may be attractive as venues for learning centers. But it would take a tremendous number of other benefits to outweigh the value of centrality.

Adjacency to other academic support resources is an important consideration. Both collaborative marketing and collaborations across units are facilitated by physical closeness, and referrals to other support resources will feel much more authentic and helpful to students when they are taken by the hand and walked there, rather than pointed to another location on a campus map.

The political ramifications of center location are also relevant. Learning centers exist to support learners rather than to serve the needs of academic departments. Positioning them within neutral spaces, trafficked by many kinds of students for many reasons, sends the message that the center is unaffiliated with departmental curricula. Locations within academic departments, or in spaces that students perceive as strongly associated with particular segments or aspects of campus, may sway students' perception of the center in ways that detract from the image it wishes to project. They may even position the center in the minds of potential users as an agent of academic programs, a participant in evaluating students rather than supporting them in rising to the demands of a curriculum.

The amount of space available within a venue is, of course, important. The size of the center is ideally determined by peak predicted use. Consider the busiest times for the center: how many students does the space need to be able to accommodate at once? For the tutoring pedagogies that your program favors, what density of seating is appropriate—that is, how close should students be to one another, and how close should groups of students involved in separate learning interactions be to one another? Taking these concerns into account, the overall size of the center should roughly be dependent on the square footage required to accommodate the appropriate number of seats, with plenty of room to navigate them comfortably.

ENTRANCE

There is no more important space in a learning center than its entrance, and no more important target for consideration of the way impression is affected by design. It is the physical reality students are presented with as they decide whether to seek the support of their peers. It's the front end and the nerve center of the program. It's the sum of the way that students who have seen the center but not yet ventured in perceive the center, and it's the point of entry for students seeking to engage with it. Kuh et al. describe the role that the physical space of learning environments plays in the student experience, fostering academic engagement and "communicat[ing] messages that influence students' feelings of well-being, belonging, and identity" (2005, p. 106). Although every aspect of center design plays a role in creating these deep, subtle ways of conveying to students their positionality with respect to the center and to the entire institution, the entryway is foremost among them.

The entrance to an academic support space has to fulfill three main functions. First, it welcomes students to the space. It should set an inviting, receptive tone. Consider the student standing at the threshold who has never used the center and is considering whether to enter. The student may be experiencing any number of factors pushing them away from the center: lack of time, fear that utilizing academic support makes them a bad student, reluctance to express vulnerability to their peers, anxiety about entering a new social space. The gravity of the center, as the student experiences through everything they perceive at the entrance, must be strong enough to counteract all of these forces pushing them away. Colors, signage, visible learning interactions, overarching design: all of these play a powerful role in student utilization and perception of the center.

The second role of the entrance is to orient students to the center. Unfamiliar spaces are fraught with ambiguities, which can easily become significant, even insurmountable obstacles for students who may experience trepidation about using the center or anxiety about entering a new social environment. No one enjoys looking like they don't know what they are doing in front of an audience. This is a particularly piquant fact for new college students (one of the most important constituencies of many learning centers), as well as for students who may experience feelings of vulnerability and self-doubt in their first moments of seeking academic support. Clear, immediately apparent, and highly accessible direction on how to access and utilize support helps students feel secure, adding to a welcoming impression and placing them in an affective state conducive to learning. Clear direction and signage provide security, helping learners not yet familiar with the center know where to log in, where to make an appointment, where to find the appropriate type of tutor/service, or where to find a restroom. Signage can provide clarity on how to use the center (e.g., "Have a question? Raise your hand, and a tutor will be by to assist you"). It can also establish social norms, clarifying the center's etiquette so the parameters for acceptable behavior are clear ("This is an academic space. Speaking and collaboration are encouraged, but we ask you to be mindful of volume and focus on study-related topics"), as well as framing the values that determine acceptable use of the space ("This center welcomes all students; it does not welcome discriminatory words or actions").

Finally, the entrance should provide a narrow, easily monitored through point for entry and exit. Tracking student utilization (discussed in more detail in chapter 9) is vital to measuring and reporting the impact and reach of the center, and a clear awareness of who is there at any given time (both learners and student employees) is frequently vital. This is only practical, in even the most moderate rush, when all traffic is channeled through a single point (or, in the case of larger centers, a few discrete points). If the center has multiple ways to enter and exit, people can and will use them. During busier times in particular, only the rare individual will wait even a few seconds in line when it's possible to walk through immediately at another point, and it quickly becomes impossible to have any accurate sense of who is making use of the center once users have become accustomed to entering and exiting the center at points other than the one being monitored.

An entry point with a desk (which ideally can be staffed by a student who welcomes those entering the space) is a common solution, providing a space where students can inquire about services, make appointments, and log in and out of sessions. It is an ideal space for signage to orient students to the center, as well as to display brochures and information for other campus resources to which students might be referred. A well-designed, inviting intake desk can anchor all of the center's advertising, sending this message to students: *if you can make it here, we have you. From this point, we'll ensure that you have the support you need, whether that support comes from within the center or from another campus program.*

The front desk of a learning center has the potential to serve as "the" stop for students, a port of entry to all of the academic support services that exist not only within the center, but across campus. This approach positions the center as the connecting hub of the campus network of academic support resources, reducing barriers to accessing those resources. In order to live up to this role, the front desk should be as easy to find and well-marked as possible. In many centers, the front desk also provides an ideal location for secure but accessible storage of resources that may be helpful to tutors and learners in the center (e.g., textbooks, course syllabi on file, electronic devices, scrap paper, spare pens).

Inclusivity is a central consideration to the entrances of learning centers. Being broadly welcoming is very much to the good. It's also important to consider to whom, specifically, the entrance to the center is welcoming. Does it assume a white, English-speaking, able-bodied, and neurotypical learner? In what ways is the entrance to the center welcoming to students representing diverse, marginalized identities? How might the imagery, design, and facilities resonate (or not) with students of color, students who are not native speakers of English, students with physical disabilities, and neurodiverse students as they enter the center? Is the signage accessible to them? Would they see their own identity represented in the images on decorations and printed materials? Is the entrance to the space designed in a way that signals that their unique needs will be taken into account there? In order to serve the entire student body, the center must present as fully welcoming to every segment of it.

LAYOUT

The space of a learning center sends clear, if implicit, messages to its users on their role within it, on how the center exists in relation to its users, and on how it should be perceived. Metz Bemer articulates the need for learning centers to create an environment in which students feel comfortable and wanted: "Student comfort means students feel self-confident in a situation. Creating a comfortable situation for tutors and students can be done through designing for one thing: choice" (2010, p. 138).

In designing the layout of a venue for peer tutoring, the overarching concern is flexibility. The site should provide learners with options as to their learning environment, driven by their preferences and by the type of work in which they are currently engaged: quiet areas and busy areas, areas for individual study and areas for collaborative learning, areas focused on comfort and areas focused on productivity. For tutors, the design of the center should provide choices to make in how to engage with learners: ways to meet with students in 1:1 consultation, ways to engage learners in small groups, and ways to facilitate larger groups of learners. Learning centers engage with students as unique learners. It's essential, in accomplishing this goal and in signaling the difference between learning centers and the one-size-fits-all, instructor-led spaces of classrooms, for learners to be able to make meaningful choices about where and how to do the work of being a student, and for tutors to be supported by the space in making intentional, pedagogy-driven choices on how to engage learners.

These choices can be fluid, occurring in the moment. How does the space support a tutor who, in circulating through a drop-in lab, notices several students working on the same problem and seeks to pull them together into a small collaborative learning session? How does the space support students who, presented with a busy center encountering peak use, find themselves distracted by the visual and auditory distractions and seek an area in which they can better concentrate? How does the space support a tutor who would like one student in a group to model a concept for her peers, creating a diagram that everyone in the group can discuss? How does the space support a student who needs a large amount of table space to lay out a large, complicated project? How does the space support a tutor working with a learner who is engaging with an online learning environment?

In all of these cases, the space of the center can either facilitate or hinder the choices that learners make and the work that tutors do. Varied spaces that present multiple options, including the option to easily rearrange the space (e.g., through separations created by furniture and movable partitions rather than by immobile partitions), make the space more responsive to the needs of its users on a day-to-day basis and more responsive to changes in programming or in patterns of use in the center.

The partition of spaces within a center and their arrangement relative to one another will vary widely between smaller centers (where all available subject areas and formats of tutoring may be available within a single room) and larger centers (where it may be necessary to impose an organization on the space in order to address logistical concerns and ease of student use). Some centers are organized by content areas (e.g., writing area, math area, science area), others by tutoring formats (e.g., individual appointment area, drop-in area, workshop area) or volume (e.g., quiet study area, collaborative learning zone). Most involve some hybrid or combination of the above. In all scenarios, the ease and comfort of student use should be the primary concern. It should be intuitive for students where to go. Learners should never have to enter a space to find, without direction, the appropriate support: either they should be guided to the appropriate area by a tutor or other student worker or led there by clear signage. The use of the center as a space for tutor training may also be a consideration for the overall organizational schema of the space. Where it's practical to do so, large areas without partitions can become spaces where all of the tutors within a center can be gathered and addressed. Discrete areas within the center create locations for breakout sessions to engage tutors in smaller groups or by disciplinary team.

FURNITURE

Furniture is a highly subtle, eloquent way of signaling to students how to use the space, both reflecting and steering pedagogy. Small tables with two chairs at them tell students that peer tutoring is a one-to-one interaction between themselves and a tutor. Chairs on the same side of a table, facing the same work surface, direct students toward the expectation that the session will be focused on shared engagement over a piece of their work or writing. Round tables with multiple chairs around them imply conversation and collaboration among groups of students. Items of furniture all send clear messages about how to operate within a space. These messages can certainly be overcome—a tutor and a student can absolutely have a one-on-one session at a large round table or a dialogic session in chairs facing the same direction. The right furniture, however, optimizes the space for the types of pedagogical interactions that the tutors are trained to engage in, and it articulates what expectations students should have about how to engage as learners within the center, and how to relate to the tutors within it.

Accessibility for wheelchair users is an essential consideration at the level of overall design and layout and comes into play particularly for furniture selection and placement. Learning centers should be welcoming to every learner, and nothing signals a lack of welcome to a wheelchair user more clearly than inadequate access. Routes for wheelchair and motorized scooter users into the center and to every area within it should be allowed for in mapping out the layout of the center, with furniture spaced to allow for easy access. Furniture options should allow for wheelchair and motorized scooter users to comfortably join groups, use table-top space and computers, and in all other ways fully participate in the models for tutoring used within the center.

ACCESSIBLE DESIGN FOR THE
PHYSICAL SPACE OF LEARNING CENTERS

Universal design specialist Sheryl Burgstahler offers the following principles for accessibility in the physical design of learning centers, ensuring that "facilities, activities, materials, and equipment are physically accessible to and usable by all students, and that all potential student characteristics are addressed in safety considerations" (2017, pp. 2–3):

- Are there parking areas, pathways, and entrances to the building that are wheelchair accessible and clearly identified?
- Are all levels of the facility connected via an accessible route of travel?
- Are there ample high-contrast, large-print directional signs to and throughout the office?
- Do elevators have auditory, visual, and tactile signals, and are elevator controls accessible from a seated position?
- Are wheelchair-accessible restrooms with well-marked signs available in or near the office?
- Is at least part of a service counter or desk accessible from a seated position?
- Are aisles kept wide and clear of obstructions for the safety of users who have mobility or visual impairments?
- Are there quiet work or meeting areas where noise and other distractions are minimized and/or facility rules in place (e.g., no cell phone use) that minimize noise?
- Is adequate light available?
- Are printed materials within easy reach from a variety of heights and without furniture blocking access?
- Is an adjustable-height table available for each type of workstation to assist students who use wheelchairs or are small or large in stature?

Variation is one important consideration in determining the appropriate furniture for a center. The presence of a variety of furniture types (small tables, larger tables, soft chairs, couches, booths, computer workstations, private carrels) creates a center that is responsive to a variety of student preferences and supportive of a variety of pedagogies. Even within a small center, variation is possible and desirable. Within a single 20' × 20' room staffed by a handful of tutors, selecting three or four different types of furniture will create far more flexibility for tutors and learners than will a homogenous selection of desks or tables.

Flexibility is another. Furniture that can be used for a variety of purposes, combined into large arrangements or separated into smaller ones allows a space to be responsive to minute-to-minute changes in the needs of tutors and students (e.g., pushing two smaller wheeled tables together to form a larger one when a large study group forms, or pulling a large area of soft seating apart into a number of smaller segments to accommodate breakout sessions).

WHITEBOARDS

Whiteboards (generally preferable to chalkboards for learning centers, because they are cleaner and less intimidating for students to use) are extremely helpful additions to peer-led learning spaces. They make it possible for tutors to easily create visual aids that can be referred to throughout a session. They allow a tutor to interact with students in groups, pulling students in around the recognizable leadership cue of a visual. They create a way for tutors to easily change the dynamic of an interaction, making a learner an active participant in the session or deflecting the role of leader/expert by asking them to create an outline, diagram, list, brainstorm, or other visual/written artifact of the session (which learners can then snap a picture of, creating a resource they can refer to later when working individually).

In a group learning environment, whiteboards provide an easy way for learners to demonstrate their own approach to solving a problem to a group, or for multiple participants to record and compare their responses to a prompt. Importantly, whiteboards can be but are not necessarily expensive purchases. Generally, the larger the whiteboard, the more expensive it will be. In a classroom setting, large whiteboards, which can hold information from a long lecture and be viewed by students at a distance, are at a premium. Within a peer tutoring environment, whiteboard sizes and configurations designed for smaller groups are generally preferable. Small whiteboards (often known as huddleboards) are, in fact, particularly useful, allowing a small group to work collaboratively on a shared task and share their work with a larger group. Portable, wheeled whiteboards are helpful in a different way, contributing to the general responsiveness of the space to changing student/tutor needs and becoming impromptu space dividers as needed.

The power dynamics that furniture and layout create are extremely important to consider. Learning centers are student spaces. As a general organizing principle, learning centers should create learner-led spaces that students can fully inhabit, making themselves comfortable as they do their work. Tutors can then enter these spaces to engage with the learner on their own terms (the antithesis of this arrangement would be a setup in which the tutor occupies a desk or table, their things arrayed on it, controlling a tutor-led space that learners must enter in order to access support). Space and furniture can be powerful signifiers of differences in power, control, and expertise: people look to the fronts of rooms and elevated platforms for figures who control spaces, acting as authorities.

For peer tutors, the role of expert is anathema: tutors are proximate models for academic behavior and facilitators of learning interactions between peers, not authority figures. The choices that you make in determining the look, feel, and design of the center are highly important—far more important than anything you say, or assign as a reading, or put on a flyer—in showing both tutors and learners how to think about the relationship between the students who work in and use the services of the center.

METAPHORS FOR LEARNING CENTER DESIGN

One powerful way of thinking about physical space of your center is to consider the types of environments that its design suggests. Learning centers will be, for most new college students and many more advanced ones, unfamiliar spaces. In a multitude of ways, too small, subtle, and numerous to address through signage, students may feel uncertain about how to navigate the center: is it a formal space, or one in which they can relax? Do they need to whisper? Can they talk to their friends, about things that aren't studying? Should they approach a tutor, or wait to be approached?

These ambiguities can make the learning center an uncomfortable space or detract from it as a learning environment. By using design choices that suggest other, more familiar environments, administrators can provide students with implicit messages about the center and how to be within it. Students may or may not be familiar with learning centers, but they are probably familiar with, for example, the environment of a coffeeshop (high-top café tables, modern decor, chalk art advertising services, counter service, a healthy buzz of activity). In suggesting this more familiar environment through choices in color, art, furniture, and layout, it is invoked as a metaphor for understanding and navigating the center, shaping the way that students will relate to it and behave within it. Within larger centers, using different metaphors to structure different areas of the center can create zones that have different "feels," each comfortable for different purposes and to different types of learners.

In selecting the metaphors that will shape the design of the center, administrators should think carefully about the mission of the center and what ways of construing it are most resonant with the identity (or desired identity) of the program. Jackie Grutsch McKinney (2005), in a critique of the common design language of writing centers as a "cozy home," encourages us to critically and carefully consider the metaphors that structure our choice of design and decor and how these may impact students' relationship to the space. She notes that an aesthetic of comfortable relaxation may be at odds with a view of the center as a place to work, and she points out as well that the notion of "home" is a culturally grounded concept that may function as effectively to exclude some students as to invite others. Karen Smith cautions learning centers against adopting the metaphor of a medical facility, with "closed-door areas much too similar to the doctor's examining room where you learn about your affliction—or academic problem—and may be given a prescription for a remedy—guidance and assistance" (2001, p. 83).

Another metaphor that is particularly important not to invoke is that of the classroom. Classrooms as spaces carry with them a highly structured set of rules and implications, in particular for the relationship between learners and educators. Learning centers stand apart from the curriculum, supporting it but providing an alternate, more student-driven approach that is not focused on the expertise of educators but on the agency of learners. Design choices that suggest classroom environments (podiums, an identifiable "front" of the room, a separate desk for the educator) send powerful, implicit messages about the role of learners in education that are antithetical to learning centers. If classroom space is the only space you have available, consider ways of moving furniture around to deflect the dynamic of learners observing the front of the room.

TECHNOLOGY

Technology can be highly supportive to the mission of a center. It can help learners connect to online resources. It can support neurodiversity and differences in ability, providing a variety of ways for diverse learners to engage with course content. It can facilitate the centers' engagement with departmental curricula, which may include components delivered via online modules. It can empower tutors to directly support the acquisition of fluency in specialized software applications and online environments. Technology can provide a way for tutors to act as guides and mentors to the larger communities of knowledge that exist in digitally mediated spaces, supporting learners in developing the skills and literacies that will allow them to fully participate in the hyperconnected landscape of modern academic and professional life. Technology can also be prohibitively expensive, a sink for resources more fruitfully applied to tutoring hours or to other resources. It can be distracting, drawing learners' cognitive resources away from their immediate academic goals and toward overcoming usability issues with hardware or applications (or toward social media). It can be transitory, the season's hot educational technology forgotten or made obsolete within a few years. For technology to be effective in the center, it can't wag the dog of actual student learning: decisions on interspersed technology should be approached as solutions to issues that have emerged in the center, not as ends in themselves. Brown and Long write:

> The unrelenting pace of technology change can make IT decisions rapidly obsolete. While platforms and applications come and go, the psychology of how people learn does not. Constructivist learning principles, specifically activities identified as encouraging learning, can be translated into design principles that guide tactical decisions, ensuring that the designs we build and the technology we deploy serve a clear educational purpose. This suggests a design methodology with a clear "genealogy" having constructivist principles as the "parent" of design principles leading to specific tactics that support and enhance learning. (2006, pp. 117–118)

Within a learning center environment, worthwhile and cost-effective educational technologies are those that directly help students to attain learning outcomes supported by the mission of the center, facilitate learning rather than function as an obstacle to it, and are demonstrably more effective than less expensive, non-technological solutions.

Several technologies have proven to be reliably helpful and useful across a wide variety of learning center applications. Tablets and laptops that can be checked out to students or tutors provide full access to software and internet to students for whom personal devices are not economically feasible. They can also support accessibility, allowing access to preinstalled text reading, magnification, voice transcription, and other software tools designed to let students with differences in ability fully access academic curricula. A few desktop computer workstations throughout a center can provide larger monitors than those available to students on personal laptops or tablets, supporting complex tasks, visual projects, and group collaboration around a single screen. They allow rapid access to online resources for tutors engaging students nearby in interactions that aren't centered around a connected device. Large, wall-mounted monitors with the ability to mirror displays from nearby devices are powerful, flexible, and relatively inexpensive. They can be used for a variety of scenarios, allowing for group collaboration around a project, a presenter-led session, or for multiple participants in a group session to show their own approach to responding to a prompt.

Many other tools are available, of course, and many more will emerge over time. Effective learning-center technology is simple (operating according to straightforward principles, or taking advantage of users' familiarity from other venues). It is multiuse, allowing tutors and learners to take advantage of it across a variety of content areas and tutoring scenarios. And it should lend itself to the core pedagogies of active learning and collaboration. Above all else, it should be either dead simple or based on technology already familiar to most students. If it's not, it won't be used. The students who use the center are there because they have a goal: they want to understand cell division, or complete their paper, or get an answer to their question about the dative. They don't want to devote time to mastering a new item of technology or figuring out how it's relevant to the work that they're doing. The same is true of tutors, who are generally operating under time constraints: if it's not immediately apparent how an item of technology will be helpful to the session, it won't be utilized. For an item of technology to be helpful in the center, its benefits have to outweigh its costs in the time it takes to set it up and utilize it and in the effort it takes to learn how to do so.

The most important principle in supporting the use of technology in the center, overriding all other considerations: provide plenty of outlets and access to a strong Wi-Fi signal. In considering the latter, be sure to work with your campus IT department to plan around peak usage. Times when the center is busiest also tend to be times when stress levels are high, and loss of access to online resources, documents in cloud storage, and course pages can completely remove students' ability to be productive there.

DECORATIONS

The wall decorations of the center are simultaneously one of the lowest-stakes aspects of design, able to be changed out easily, frequently, and at little cost (even moved easily between borrowed spaces), and one of the most essential, contributing to the overall look and feel of the center greatly disproportionate to the cost and effort they entail. The decorations are an opportunity to model the pedagogies used in the center (e.g., with images of students involved in the types of learning interactions that you hope will unfold in the center) and the attitude toward the endeavor of learning that you aim to have the center impart (e.g., images and quotes from tutors, students, public intellectuals, or advanced disciplinary learners, writers, and thinkers). They express the vision and mission of the center (perhaps literally, as large displays of the center's vision and mission can make excellent contributions to the center's décor, placing the values that motivate the tutors' work front and center). They can signal the receptiveness of the center toward a diverse student body and its active allyship toward students from marginalized groups. They can play a role in creating a calming, stress-reducing space that helps to optimize the mental and emotional state for learning. They can create, through words and pictures, a tone for the center as a thriving, social, supportive, welcoming, challenging, and intellectually engaging space.

The decorations can showcase the contributions of the tutors who work within it. The walls of the center are an ideal home for projects that tutors create, as well as images (perhaps accompanied by quotations) of current and former tutors. Displays of student scholarship on peer tutoring and other aspects of the study of teaching and learning (drawn with tutors' permission from assignments in peer tutor courses and training programs) help to foster an academic tone and demonstrate clearly to faculty and administration visitors that learning-center theory is a domain of scholarly inquiry and the work in which peer tutors engage is highly informed by current best practices.

Decorations are also an incredible way to increase student agency in the space. Every opportunity for students to create informal art within the center (chalk art, doodles on whiteboards, "quotes of the day" or other messages on a display dedicated to the sole purpose of decoration), even (or perhaps especially) when it has nothing to do with tutoring or learning, is an opportunity to show the center as a student-led space, with a culture set and defined by the learners and tutors within it rather than by center leadership or by the larger institution. More broadly, the more control tutors have within a space, the greater sense of investment they will have within it. Providing your tutors with a voice in the overall look and feel of the center not only will create a greater sense of agency for tutors, but it also likely will create a tone for the center that is more resonant for learners than would be accomplished by the strict control of a professional staff. Decorations provide students with a voice in overall design while accommodating a changing vision and contributions of successive cohorts of tutors. A system for easily and quickly changing decorations without undue effort or damage to walls (e.g., a strip of cork running the perimeter of the room, or frames the images within which can be periodically replaced) can be helpful to consider in (re)designing the space of the learning center.

At the same time, decoration should not be overdone. Graetz (2006, p. 74), describing the way students operate within learning spaces, notes that "Students cannot attend to all the environmental information bombarding them at any given time; their ability to gather and understand incoming information is limited." Signage and decorations are an important aspect of supporting the accessibility and affective impact of the space, but they should be balanced against the need to support students in devoting cognitive resources to their studies. It should be sufficient (and sufficiently visible) to accomplish its intended purpose but not so pervasive in the environment as to become a cognitive distraction to students who are struggling with a complex task or are predisposed to be diverted by excessive stimuli within their visual field.

The way learning interactions will unfold within the learning center is complex, dynamic, and emergent. You have, at your disposal, a variety of ways to influence the character and dynamic of the center, affecting the way that the students within it relate to one another. The design of the physical space of the center is one of the most subtle and powerful.

QUESTIONS FOR PROGRAM ASSESSMENT

Location

- Is the center located where it is visible and easily accessible for the target student population?
- Is the center situated in reasonable proximity to complementary academic support services?
- Is the center situated in a space that students will perceived as neutral (unaffiliated with any particular academic program of study)?
- Is the size of the center adequate to the needs of the program, allowing tutors to engage students using the pedagogical approaches the program favors at times of peak usage?

Entrance

- Is the entrance to the center welcoming and inviting, including for students representing marginalized identities?
- Does the entrance provide clear orientation (especially for new users) on how to use the center?
- Does the entrance provide a narrow, easily monitored point of access that allows for tracking student utilization?

Layout

- Does the layout of the center provide learners with options for their learning environment?
- Does the layout provide tutors with flexibility in how they engage learners, supporting them in making empowered choices about pedagogical approaches?
- Is the overall space organized in a way that is intuitive for learners?

Furniture

- Does the furniture used within the center support and empower the specific pedagogies/modes of interaction between learners, and between tutors and learners, used in your center?
- Do the choice and arrangement of furniture allow for full participation for wheelchair users and individuals of varying height in every aspect of the center?
- Is the furniture varied, providing tutors and learners with meaningful choices?
- Does the furniture arrangement allow for minute-to-minute and long-term changes in patterns of student usage?
- Does the furniture arrangement within the center suggest a power dynamic in which tutors and learners are equal participants in the learning process?

Technology

- Does the infrastructure of the center allow users of personal devices adequate access to power and data?
- Does the technology available within the center provide full access for learners who may not have access to personal devices to fully participate in center programming and in online communities of knowledge?
- Does the technology support diversity, allowing learners who may vary in neurological and physical ability to fully participate in center programming and in online communities of knowledge?
- Is the technology intuitive for tutors and learners?

Decorations

- Do the decorations in the center align with its values, mission, and desired image?
- Do the decorations help to create an environment conducive to learning?
- Do the decorations reflect tutors' agency in setting the tone for the space?

Signage

- Does the signage in the center align with the brand conveyed in marketing materials?
- Does the signage provide clarity for learners on how to access services offered within the center?
- Does the signage provide clarity for learners on the cultural norms of the space?
- Is the signage as minimal and succinct as possible to accomplish its purpose?

Chapter Seven

Collaborating with Campus Partners

Collaboration is a core strategy in learning-center administration and a defining aspect of what a learning center is. Collaboration makes it possible to extend the reach of the center, building bridges to student populations who may not have the comfort, self-advocacy, or prerequisite knowledge of campus resources to seek out peer tutoring. It leverages the expertise of colleagues with insight on the needs of specific groups of learners. And it allows for time, money, skill, and other resources that would otherwise exist in separate institutional silos to be combined in ways that maximize their impact on student success.

Collaboration is possible in the space where missions intersect. Although every student-oriented unit is a potential collaborator, and every campus program supports, in some way, the overarching mission of the institution, the most promising potential partners are departments and programs with missions oriented around students' academic success. Where missions converge, and where care is taken to develop healthy partnerships, the different approaches to (and even lenses for understanding) student success that occur in different units (and in different professional communities) can complement one another, mutually enriching each other and deeply strengthening the campus support networks that allow every student to persist—and, further, to thrive—in their studies.

COLLABORATIONS WITH ACADEMIC DEPARTMENTS

Academic departments and learning centers exist in a complex relationship with one another. On the one hand, academic departments are learning centers' closest partners, with goals that align with those of the center: to retain students in their intended major; to support them in graduating in a timely manner; to create students who are successful learners, thinkers, writers, and problem solvers in the academic disciplines; to foster students' success in individual courses and, moreover, their ability to transfer skills and knowledge across courses to succeed in the overall curriculum. On the other hand, differences in philosophy and pedagogical approach between classroom instruction and peer-led learning, as well as misunderstandings about the learning center's role on campus (e.g., that its purpose is remedial instruction, that tutors' role is to check students' work so that they hand in perfect assignments, that peer tutoring comprises advanced students explaining concepts to less advanced students) can result in significant tensions between LCAs and departments and/or individual instructors.

Institutional power structures pertaining to differences in position status (e.g., between faculty and staff, or between tenure-track and non-tenure-track faculty) may come into play as well, with some classroom instructors perhaps failing to appreciate the value that learning centers add to institutions, and the insight and expertise that LCAs bring to collaborations around student learning. Academic departments are nonetheless absolutely indispensable partners for learning centers.

Faculty within departments are able to provide insight into academic curricula, including "sticking points" where students often struggle, as well as provide strategically important information on upcoming changes to courses that LCAs can account for in their planning. They are critical in making hiring recommendations, able to speak to students in their courses who are competent and confident with course material and who may have emerged as natural leaders within their courses. They can provide information on upcoming assessments (exams, papers, etc.) to be used in short-term planning, staffing for anticipated rushes of students, and preparing tutors to address specific issues. They can help to create connections between the learning center and classroom by inviting tutors to present on the center or to lead classroom activities. They can be partners in creating new programming initiatives, collaborations that incorporate models of peer-led tutoring (see chapter 3) that support the needs of students in their courses.

Above all else, they are (or can be) the greatest ally of the center in referring students for tutoring, ensuring that students who could benefit from using the services of the center are encouraged to do so. The faculty is an incredible source of guest speakers for tutor trainings, able to speak both to strategies for learners to work through challenging concepts in the disciplines and to disciplinary approaches to learning that can be more broadly applied in learning centers. Creating and maintaining healthy collaborations with academic departments is one of the most important responsibilities of LCAs in ensuring that the benefits of peer tutoring are realized for students within academic curricula and that peer tutors are set up to succeed in their work with learners.

SESSION NOTES

Some centers adopt the practice of having tutors take notes on sessions with learners. Sometimes used for assessment purposes (e.g., to gather information on recurring themes in sessions, or to track individual learner's growth over time), such notes generally gather information on the issue(s) that brought a student to the center, what took place during a session, and the outcomes of the session. Such a system is generally only practical in centers that operate on an individual appointment model, which creates breaks between appointments that tutors can use to decompress sessions. In some variations of the practice, session notes are created collaboratively between tutors and students as a way to close the session.

Such session notes can be a flash point in relationships between learning centers administrators and faculty in academic departments. Whereas LCAs tend to view themselves as advocates for students and for their right to privacy, faculty may feel a right to information regarding their students' use of the center in connection with courses that they teach. For every learning center, it's important to articulate a clear policy, in accord with the mission of the center and with respect for students' rights to control information on their use of the center, that clearly dictates what information the center shares with faculty and in what circumstances it does so. For centers that retain notes on sessions, this issue is particularly piquant, as the question arises of whether (and, again, in what circumstances) such records can be shared with faculty.

A good practice to follow regarding the sharing of any information on students' use of the center is to place students in firm control of what information they would like to be shared with their instructors (e.g., by requiring explicit permission from students to share information and to determine what information they want shared). Although faculty are important allies in the work of learning centers, learning centers are not agents of academic departments—it's essential for learners to view the learning center not as an extension of the classroom in which their performance is graded, but as a separate space where they have the freedom to do the work of being in a student in a supported, low-stakes, environment, free of any thought of how instructors will view and assess their efforts.

The key to productive relationships with academic departments is for faculty to have a clear idea of what the center is and does. The challenge in doing so is that faculty are often busy (teaching, engaging in research, and attending to their institutional service obligations) and narrowly focused (on the concerns of their own department, students, and scholarly agenda). It can be challenging to capture the attention of faculty members sufficiently to convey a clear picture of the work of the center. Moreover, faculty members who have been in their positions for many years (and who may also, for precisely this reason, have a large amount of influence over their peers and students) may have an understanding of the learning center that is rooted in previous iterations of academic support structures and older models of peer tutoring. However, the role of course instructors in shaping how students perceive the learning center cannot be overstated. An enthusiastic endorsement of the learning center to their course from an instructor can be instrumental in encouraging a healthy relationship with academic support for their students. A single dismissive comment or misguided recommendation can all but guarantee that a student will perceive the center in a way (as remedial, as not helpful, as unnecessary, as a lesser substitute for office hours, as the domain of unintelligent students) that will prevent them from making use of it in that or any other course.

It's critical that all faculty have a basic idea of what services the center provides, the relevance of those services to the courses that they teach, and

OFFERING CREDIT/EXTRA CREDIT FOR TUTORING

An issue that commonly arises for LCAs is the question of whether to allow instructors to require their students to access tutoring as a course requirement, or to offer extra credit to students who utilize the services of the center. Both sides of the issue bear important considerations to weigh in determining a policy (issues that have been explored at some length in writing center scholarship—see, e.g., Bell & Stutts, 1997; Bishop, 1990; Bourelle, 2007; Clark, 1985; Gordon, 2008; Osman, 2007; Rendleman, 2013).

On the one hand, requiring/offering extra credit for tutoring incentivizes the use of the center. This creates an opportunity for tutors, working with learners who may not otherwise have used tutoring, to make the case that the center is a helpful service. It also creates the potential for correcting learners' possible misconceptions about the center, replacing an erroneous or incomplete understanding of academic support with a more nuanced and accurate view. Hopefully, these experiences will persuade learners of the utility of accessing the center as an academic habit.

On the other hand, required/extra credit sessions can create a challenging dynamic in tutoring sessions. Tutors working with students who are present in the center not because of innate motivation but because they received an incentive to do so often report learners who are unengaged or unresponsive in the session. In addition, for instructors to be able to give credit for tutoring, there needs to be some form of reporting on the part of the center, providing information on which instructors' students used the center during a given time period. This requires a level of logistic consideration and has an ethical component: it reduces students' agency in controlling access to information on their use of academic support. This question has no one right answer, only solutions that work for individual centers.

of appropriate scenarios for referring students to the center. It's also highly valuable for faculty in the disciplines to have a clear idea of the hiring goals of the center and of the type of student that is a strong candidate to be a tutor (see chapter 4). This information should be transmitted through as many channels, and with as much repetition, as possible.

E-mails to faculty listservs (as well as center brochures sent directly to faculty mailboxes) at the beginning of each term with information on center hours and services, suggested syllabus language, and possible ways of partnering with the center are an excellent way to reach a large number of faculty as they are in the thick of preparing for the semester, considering ways to make their courses successful. Presentations to campus-wide or divisional faculty meetings, as well as visits to departmental meetings to carefully talk through scenarios in which the center may be useful for students in the program, answer questions, and discuss opportunities for collaboration, are indispensable ways of creating a deeper understanding of the center. "Absent professor programs" that offer in-class workshops that the learning center provides on days when instructors would otherwise need to cancel class due to a foreseen absence (e.g., Dawson, 2009), as well as programs to invite faculty to hold a portion of their office hours in the learning center, are opportunities to create both goodwill toward, investment in, and awareness of the center among faculty, as well as to provide a bridge for students from the classroom to the learning center.

Perhaps most important: cultivate allies. You can never reach everyone. But if you have one or two professors in each department who fully understand the mission of the center and are enthusiastic supporters, then the center has ambassadors in every large faculty gathering that takes place on campus.

COLLABORATIONS WITH ACADEMIC ADVISORS

Academic advisors help students set academic goals and support them in achieving those goals, helping students navigate the complex networks of requirements and resources that comprise institutions of higher education. Advising programs are natural allies for learning centers. While learning centers are focused on ensuring that students have the support to succeed within their courses and a growing awareness of their own academic habits as they progress between them, offices of academic advising are focused on supporting students in navigating academic curricula and moving toward their personal and professional goals. Although using different models for engaging with learners and focusing on different aspects of student development, learning centers and advising programs share goals at both the broadest scale (self-discovery, self-efficacy, and self-awareness on the part of learners), and at the level of specific outcomes (persistence, retention, and timely graduation).

Academic advisors are some of the most important partners that LCAs have on campus, because they have the relationships with students to identify times and situations in which the learning center is an appropriate intervention, even (and especially) in situations when the student would not otherwise know about campus resources or have the prerequisite self-efficacy to seek out academic support for themselves. Academic advisors interact with every student on campus. Because they have a vested interest in the same essential goals that drive the work of learning centers, they have every reason in the world to act as advocates for the center.

This can only happen, however, if advisors have in-depth knowledge of the center. It's essential that academic advisors have complete, up-to-date information on the suite of services that the center provides (including when and how they are offered), and a complex, robust understanding of how center services work. Every campus advising center should be well-stocked with brochures or other center materials that can be easily handed to students; and every advisor should mirror the language used in these brochures and by the learning center to provide students a cohesive bridge from advising to tutoring.

Through joint meetings, regular e-mail communications, interactive trainings, and/or tours of the center, academic advisors should understand the core pedagogy and target audience of the programs or services that comprise the center and the scenarios in which they might refer a student to different aspects of the center. Academic advisors often work with students who demonstrate a lack of competence in overarching skills for academic success, such as time management, note taking, or critical reading. Knowing the ways in which the center can support learners in these areas can be powerful drivers of connections between the students who need support in these areas and programming that can provide it. Academic advisors also can, if they have sufficiently fine-grained knowledge of the center, let students know what to expect when they visit the center: who the tutors are, how to make an appointment, and how to prepare for a session.

Academic advisors are also ideal advisors for learning centers on developing new programming initiatives (workshop series, tutoring locations, formats for services, etc.) because they have unique insight into the challenges that students face as they progress (or fail to progress) through academic curricula. Advisors are a critical source of information for LCAs on what students need, what programming gaps exist on campus, and what interventions would help students to progress smoothly toward a timely graduation. They can also provide feedback on why students don't use the center, or on their experiences (positive or negative) in doing so.

EARLY ALERT SYSTEMS

Early alert systems are software programs (either developed locally or purchased as an enterprise system from a vendor) designed to connect students who stand to benefit from support programming with appropriate institutional resources. Generally, early alert systems function by allowing faculty and others who interact with students to create "alerts" that flag a student as having a particular type of need, which initiates a process of proactively connecting students with the most appropriate intervention (e.g., academic support, counseling, advising). Often, early alert systems also include automated flags, creating alerts based on attendance or grade data. Early alert systems generally align with an intrusive/proactive advising approach, in that they facilitate a proactive approach to identifying and removing barriers to success (Earl, 1988; Schmitz & Andreozzi, 1990). Early alert systems are rapidly becoming the norm at public, private, and 2-year institutions alike (Habley, Bloom, & Robbins, 2012; Simons, 2011).

The evidence is somewhat mixed on the effectiveness of early alert systems in improving institutional retention and graduation rates, some studies failing to show a clear-cut benefit (Eimers, 2000; Pfleging, 2002) while others seem to indicate that early alert systems are an effective way of connecting at-risk students to needed support (Cai, Lewis, & Higdon, 2015; Deacon et al., 2017; Hudson, 2006; Tampke, 2013). It's clear that in and of themselves, they don't create student success (in fact, in an ACT [2010] report of more than one thousand institutions, both tutoring and supplemental instruction outranked early alert systems as tools for increasing retention). The participation of learning centers as active partners is absolutely essential to the success of early alert systems, which ultimately are simply a method for connecting students demonstrating signs of potential trouble to effective support resources such as tutoring, mentoring, and coaching.

In collaborating with an institutional early alert system, it's essential for learning centers to ensure that accurate information on the center is represented in the system, that faculty and other referrers have sufficient knowledge of the center to understand when it is an appropriate intervention, and that individuals who are responsible for acting on alerts (e.g., advisors or counselors) by connecting students to specific resources have a full, complex understanding of the support available through the center. Close collaboration with those in charge of the alert system ensures an intentional outreach process for every type of alert/referral that can be raised. LCAs should try to take as proactive an approach as possible, reaching out to students referred for tutoring, SI, mentoring, or other services offered through the center with a warm invitation and full information on how to access support.

COLLABORATIONS WITH LIBRARIES

The purview of librarians, in their role in higher education as educators, is information literacy. The Association of College and Research Libraries (2000) articulates the goals of academic librarians as to provide the support for students to determine what information they need, access it quickly, evaluate it critically, and use it both effectively and ethically (pp. 8–14). These are critical aspects of the work that peer tutors engage in with learners, helping them to accomplish academic tasks, build self-efficacy, learn effectively, and grow as thinkers and researchers within their chosen field(s) of study. Academic librarians and peer tutors engage in deeply complementary work with learners, peer tutors often working to support learners engaged in projects that involve (either predicated upon, or evidencing, or opportunities to develop) their information literacy. Close relationships with libraries create plentiful opportunities for collaboration (e.g., a writing center and research librarian working together to create a student workshop on effective research practices for students in a particular discipline) and mutual referral (a tutor working with a learner on a research project referring a learner to a research librarian for support with finding relevant sources, or a librarian referring a student to a tutor for support in using a software tool).

The most common collaboration between learning centers and libraries involves sharing space (Toms and Reedy's [2016] survey of learning centers places the percentage of learning centers located within campus libraries at 31%, whereas the National Census of Writing places the percentage of writing centers located within libraries at 34%). Learning centers provide accessibility, a student-oriented mind-set, a constant flow of students, and an active, engaged, peer-led learning environment: highly sought-after assets in the modern college library. Libraries provide learning centers with access to resources (both information and technology) well beyond the reach of most learning centers' budgets and a connection to one of the most deeply embedded aspects of the student experience.

The placement of learning centers within libraries creates many opportunities for closer collaborations in programming and referrals, as well as opening up the possibility of significant resource sharing (e.g., a library housing its copies of textbooks adjacent to the learning center where they can be used as a resource in tutoring sessions, or placing computers with statistical software in the learning center so that tutors can support students as they use them for quantitative analyses). For every LCA, it's important to cultivate relationships with librarians who provide access to the information and technology resources housed within libraries and that enrich learning centers with librarians' expertise on using them. For the LCA of a center housed within a library it's all the more important to do (as well as to be a good steward of library resources).

COLLABORATIONS WITH RESOURCE CENTERS

Many campus offices and organizations have missions focused on supporting specific groups of students. Ethnic and racial centers, offices for student veterans, LGBTQ student services, international students, women's centers: all of these (and many other) types of offices exist to support the needs of students who have a unique set of associated concerns and who benefit from dedicated programming. Such programs play an important role on campuses, providing individuals from groups that have been traditionally disenfranchised in higher education (and who may feel "othered" by the overarching campus culture) with spaces in which they can be fully comfortable and that also serve as sites for advocacy on campus for the needs of students from those groups. For learning centers, such programs are among the most powerful opportunities for collaboration, providing a chance to build relationships with students who may feel more comfortable within the space provided by a resource center than within the learning center and with professionals who have unique insight into the needs of specific groups of students.

Programming is a central aspect of successful collaborations between resource centers and learning centers. Study groups, individual appointments, drop-in labs, workshops, exam reviews or other interventions offered in resource centers, planned in collaboration with the staff and students of the center, can provide support that is particularly responsive to the needs of the learners that the resource center targets. Such collaborations offer incredible benefit for learning centers. They provide access to (and the opportunity to build trust with) student populations who are very likely to feel, as a member of a traditionally disenfranchised group, a sense of alienation from the institution as a whole——an alienation that may well extend to institutional programs such as learning centers. Programming (as well other forms of regular presence within resource centers, such as attendance at events that the resource center hosts) provides a bridge for students that the resource center targets to the larger learning center, making it far likelier that students will take advantage of the larger suite of programming that the learning center offers in its main locations. Ideally, the collaboration allows students that resource centers serve to share perceptions they may hold of the learning center, providing the center with valuable input toward changes in the space, programming, marketing, or even the central mission of the center.

The exchange of expertise is, to no less an extent, a critical aspect of successful collaborations between resource centers and learning centers. LCAs and peer tutors bring a set of skills and pedagogies related to learning center theory and administration (peer-led learning, student leadership, academic skills, assessment of student learning, student success) that are valuable for any student-facing program and every other aspect of learning center theory. The staff of student resource centers offer equally essential expertise: insight on the unique needs of students from the group that the center targets.

Learning centers purport to respond to students as unique learners in a way that reflects the diverse identities that students bring to the academy. Student resource centers are the best possible resource for insight, grounded in both scholarship and in the local social landscape, on concerns, issues, tools, and strategies for supporting students from the group(s) in question in their growth as learners. Training on tutoring across diversity is essential preparation for all tutors. Time spent within student resource centers is an opportunity for tutors to practice and develop these skills, as well as to gain perspective on the lived experience on campus of students who may represent backgrounds that differ from their own. Tutor trainings are another space for this expertise to be relayed. The professional staff of student resource centers are an ideal source of expertise on the needs of learners from particular groups. Having representatives of student resource centers as regular guest trainers provide insight for tutors about what it is to be a member of the group(s) they serve, the experience of that group in higher education, and successful strategies for addressing their unique needs, is an exceptionally productive outcome of a successful collaboration.

The most valuable source of insight and experience on a diverse student body is diverse students themselves. Student resource centers are outstanding first stops for hiring announcements, solicitations for tutor nominations, and hiring fairs. The most important way to create a tutoring staff informed by diverse perspectives and welcoming to diverse learners is to build a tutoring staff that is itself diverse. Student resource centers are essential partners in doing so.

FUNDING COLLABORATIONS

One common and productive form of collaboration between learning centers and other campus units is for a unit with a vested interest in the academic success of a specific group of students (e.g., an athletics program, or a particular program or college within the larger institution) to offer funding for the learning center to provide academic support (often at a dedicated location) for those students. For the funding units, such collaborations are both efficacious (allowing them to realize the benefits of best practices in hiring and training peer educators) and cost-effective (freeing them overhead expenses for peer tutoring and allocating all available funds directly to tutoring). For learning centers, these collaborations provide additional resources and additional opportunities to connect with particular groups of students. They may also provide additional sites for tutoring that, in turn, include more options for learners to access the learning center.

Total clarity regarding the terms of the agreement being entered into is absolutely essential in funding collaborations. Creating a memorandum of understanding that both units sign, clearly spelling out all aspects of the agreement, is both a beneficial exercise in joint planning and a way for both units to clearly understand their obligations under the agreement—and the consequences if expectations are not met. Questions to be answered include: Is the partner unit requesting a specific number of hours of programming? What happens if requests for changes are made in the middle of a term? Is the partner unit funding only student hours spent in tutoring, or their hours in training as well? What is the role of the partner unit in hiring tutors? How will funding transfers be handled? What regular reporting will the learning center create? If space is provided, what does supervision look like for the tutors in the allocated space? What physical resources will each party provide?

The golden rule for funding collaborations between learning centers and other programs is that all programming offered under the auspices of the learning center must be available for all students so it can enrich the center's overall offerings available to any student on campus. Although the particular set of students who are the purview of the partner program (e.g., student athletes, engineering students, international students) may be the focus—even the primary beneficiaries of service that the learning center provides under the agreement—the programming that the collaboration funds should be implemented in a way that makes it available for all learners, forms a whole with the larger suite of programming the center offers, and follows the same fundamental approach/pedagogy as other center services.

COLLABORATIONS WITH
ACCESSIBILITY RESOURCE CENTERS

Accessibility resource centers are programs dedicated to supporting the needs of students with disabilities. Broadly tasked with ensuring that college students have all of the protections guaranteed under federal laws (such as, in the United States, the 1990 Americans with Disabilities Act), accessibility resource centers provide resources and support for students with physical and cognitive disabilities. In many cases, they also provide testing services for students to ascertain whether they have disabilities that qualify them for accommodations allowing them to fully access the breadth of services that the college or university provides and play a role in alerting campus entities of their responsibilities in implementing such accommodations (e.g., alerting a faculty member of a student's need for extra time to complete examinations). Importantly, accessibility resource centers often also serve as sites for advocacy on college campuses, for the rights of students with disabilities to full participation within the institution and for the responsibility of educators and administrators to implement curricula and programming in a way that is fully inclusive of students encompassing a diverse spectrum of physical and cognitive abilities.

Accessibility resource centers are extremely valuable partners for collaboration, offering expertise that empowers learning centers to fulfill their mission to support every learner. Cultivating a close relationship with the campus accessibility resource center provides an LCA with a contact that can be used as a source of advice and guidance in attending to the needs of neurodiverse learners, either on a case-by-case basis or on matters of center policy (e.g., seeking input on how a writing tutor can best support a repeat user who has dyslexia, or how a content tutor can best support the needs of students with attention deficit disorder).

They can serve as consultants on accessibility, ensuring that the center is meeting its legal and ethical obligations to ensure that the physical space, materials, and programming of the center are all fully accessible for students with disabilities. Further, they can advise on universal design (Rose & Meyer, 2002; Story, Mace, & Mueller, 1998), ensuring that the physical and virtual presence of the center is designed in a way that makes the needs of physically and cognitively diverse learners a central concern and simultaneously improves the experience of all users. They can advise the center on (and potentially also provide access to) assistive technology that can be used to help students with disabilities accomplish academic tasks, and that tutors may use to interact with learners when a disability creates challenges in communication. As guest trainers, they can provide guidance for tutors on how to be mindful of the needs of physically and cognitively diverse learners, scenarios in which it may be appropriate to seek additional support from the accessibility resource center, and issues of privacy and sensitivity in working with learners who may have disabilities.

A close relationship between the campus learning center and accessibility resource center is valuable for the latter as well, providing an additional form of support to which students with disabilities can be referred. For many neurodiverse learners, peer tutoring is an ideal intervention because it offers more customized support and fewer time constraints than other forms of instruction. Programming related to learning strategies is particularly helpful for professionals working in accessibility resource centers to know about and have access to, because many disabilities related to processing and executive control materialize as issues with students' time management, planning, and strategies for learning.

COLLABORATIONS WITH CENTERS FOR COUNSELING AND MENTAL HEALTH

Centers for counseling and mental health support students' capacity for growth, learning, and development by attending to their emotional well-being. Like learning centers, such programs often have a combination of services available for students who actively seek them (e.g., individual counseling sessions) and proactive programming designed to make an impact on the student body at large (e.g., workshops on how to make healthy choices). Like learning centers, counseling and mental health centers are often focused in their marketing and outreach on making sure that students have an accurate idea of the center and the services it provides so that in moments of crisis when students urgently need such services, they know that they are available and how to access them. And like learning centers, counseling and mental health centers are highly dependent on the role that faculty, advisors, and academic staff play in referring students for support in appropriate scenarios.

Peer tutoring often involves a close, trusting relationship between tutors and learners. Because of this, and also because of the lack of a power differential between tutors and learners, students often feel comfortable disclosing aspects of their personal experience that they may not feel comfortable disclosing to an adviser, teacher, or someone else perceived as an authority figure. Tutors are very often privy to highly personal revelations from the students who they work with. A close partnership with campus counseling and mental health centers is the key to ensuring that tutors handle such disclosures appropriately and that students who a need the services of a mental health professional are connected to appropriate support.

For counseling and mental health centers, learning centers can be an incredibly valuable first line of identifying students who may have experienced a recent trauma, who may be experiencing anxiety or depression, who may be struggling with addiction, who are manifesting symptoms of a potential mental illness, or who are in any way experiencing challenges to their emotional well-being. The professionals who work within counseling and mental health centers can provide support for tutors (either directly in tutor trainings, or indirectly through guidance communicated through an LCA) on identifying scenarios in which a referral is appropriate and handling such scenarios ethically, legally, discreetly, and with consideration for the well-being both of the learner and tutor involved.

Very often, counseling and mental health centers are excellent resources not only on making referrals to their services, but on other aspects of the overlap between learning centers and counseling and mental health centers. The counselors, psychiatrists, social workers, and other professionals who work within counseling and mental health centers are an invaluable resource as potential advisors and guest trainers on techniques for active listening, building trust, navigating uncomfortable scenarios, identifying (and pointing out) counterproductive behaviors, and other aspects of pedagogy that consider learners as full, complex, emotional beings. They can guide tutors toward greater self-awareness of their roles as models of healthy student behaviors and consideration of the ways that they can support learners in making choices that work in favor of their own academic success and overall well-being. They can also guide tutors in balancing the multiple competing demands on their time, managing stress, and bringing their best selves to their work both as educators and as students.

Counseling and mental health centers should also be considered as programming partners. Both learning centers and counseling/mental health centers have a stake in working toward a student body composed of learners who makes good choices, solve problems effectively, and maximize their personal potential for growth. Joint workshops, outreach events, and other activities are all opportunities to combine resources to work together toward these goals.

COLLABORATIONS WITH OTHER LEARNING CENTERS

On many campuses, multiple learning centers exist, each specializing in different areas of the curriculum and/or different academic skills (a scenario discussed in more detail in chapter 2). In one common constellation of academic support, for example, peer tutoring programs focused on content tutoring and academic skills exist as organizationally discrete centers from peer tutoring programs focused on writing and speaking. Supplemental instruction programs, centers for mathematical and quantitative reasoning, language learning centers, and other types of programs that incorporate peer support likewise may all exist as independent programs. Similarly, peer tutoring programs focused on supporting the needs of specific populations (e.g., student athletes, students in the natural sciences, students of color) may exist as separate centers. In such scenarios, collaboration across centers is critical in ensuring that students receive, to the absolute greatest extent possible, seamless and comprehensive academic support despite the splintering of this support across multiple centers.

Collaboration is the most straightforward when missions are complementary, with each center charged with substantially different outcomes (e.g., one center aims to support students as writers, helping them to master disciplinary modes of writing and speaking, while the other center strives to support them as learners, helping them to master disciplinary modes of problem solving and critical thinking). When centers with a complementary mission collaborate, the goal is to work together toward shared goals, with each center contributing according to its areas of specialization and expertise. This is only possible when every LCA and every peer tutor within each individual center has a full, complex understanding of the services that the other provides, allowing for creative thinking on how centers can work together toward increased student success, for cooperation in ensuring that all students are connected to the most relevant support for their unique needs, and for clear communication in addressing the needs of learners that span the missions of multiple centers.

Meetings between the professional staffs of complementary centers, with the purpose of developing a detailed understanding of the mission, services, structure and goals of the others so that all parties can think collaboratively about ways of working together to ensure that every student on campus has access to full, robust academic support, are one way to accomplish this goal. Another is joint trainings or other get-togethers between peer tutors from each center, which provide a forum for tutors to build a sense of community and shared purpose, to think about ways of collaborating across organizational boundaries in a way that supports both centers' missions, and to consider scenarios in which learners might be productively referred to another center for support.

Collaboration can be more challenging in situations where missions overlap. This may arise because one center's mission nests within the mission of another's (e.g., one center supports all students on campus, another supports students in a specific major or college), or because different centers support students in different ways in service of the same goals (e.g., one center supports student success with individual and drop-in appointments, another with supplemental instruction). Such situations can foster competition between programs for limited resources, student usage, and momentum in creating a well-regarded, growing, and effective center. Students are in no way well-served by territorialism between competing centers.

Where missions overlap, the best possible solution for students—and by extension, the best possible course of action for us as LCAs—is to combine resources in such a way that forms of support that multiple centers offer all converge on learners in a way that they experience positively. Regular strategy meetings between professional staffs on how resources can be jointly deployed in the way most beneficial for students are a prerequisite to healthy collaboration. Collaborations around training (with centers working together to create a training program that serves multiple groups of peer educators) are a particularly productive way for centers with overlapping missions to avoid replicating one another's efforts in a wasteful way.

Even in those rare cases in which the allocation of resources truly is a zero-sum game, with two or more centers in direct competition over limited funding, staff lines, and other assets, collaboration is the best path forward. Taking leadership to ensure that all tutors on campus are trained effectively, that all students on campus receive effective support, and that discrete centers are working in concert toward shared goals is the best possible way for one's program to be widely viewed as an integral part of the institution's strategic plans to support its students.

When multiple learning centers exist on a single campus, what's most important is that students understand their reasons for choosing one over another in specific scenarios and have a clear idea of how to access peer tutoring. The more confusing it is to access academic support, the less any given student will take advantage of it. Learning centers owe it to the students that we serve to work together (e.g., through shared campaigns to create awareness for students of the various forms of support available to them) to create clarity for students as to where, when, why, and how to access peer tutoring (even when the overarching structures for academic support implemented by institutional leadership fail to do so), and to create a strong culture of academic support that ultimately benefits all learners, and each of the individual centers as well.

COLLABORATION WITH ADMINISTRATION

Collaboration with administration, the art of "managing up," is an indispensable skill in learning center administration. Healthy, thriving centers are adequately funded to accomplish their mission. They have sufficient (and sufficiently skilled) professional staff and/or faculty to effectively hire, train, and coordinate the center's cohort of peer tutors and accomplish all aspects of center administration. They have physical spaces that accommodate the full range of programming offered by the center and empower students as learners. They are included in and engaged with institutional planning, critical components in colleges' and universities' plans to maintain or move toward outstanding support to succeed for every student on campus. None of this is possible without a healthy two-way relationship between the learning center and institutional (or divisional) administration, each with a clear sense of how the mission of the center supports the mission of the larger institution and of how each can best support the other.

The starting point for all healthy collaborations with institutional leadership is effective assessment. Assessment and reporting (see chapter 9) that speak to ways that the center makes effective use of funding, has a tangible impact on campus, and supports institutional outcomes is indispensable in establishing productive communication. Administrators delegate resources in the service of achieving goals. Assessment reporting speaking to the ways that the center is addressing goals the administration is interested in advancing is the most important tool LCAs have for establishing collaborations in which learning centers are recognized as powerful partners in achieving long-term strategic goals and have priority in the assignment of resources because they've demonstrated the role that they play in doing so. Meetings, presentations, regular reporting, and out-of-the-blue e-mails are all opportunities to show the impact that the learning center has on moving the needle in the precise areas that the administrator in question is focused.

FUNDING REQUESTS

Making requests for additional funding (to develop new initiatives, to offset increasing costs, to expand on successful programming, to address increased demand from students, or for any other reason) is a recurring essential component of learning center administration. Learning centers accomplish work that is vital to students and to institutions, but in making requests for additional funding, are competing with many other worthy, persuasive requests. For a request to have the best possible chance of approval, it's important to follow a few general guidelines.

Be clear. Lead with the specific amount that is being requested and the use to which the funds will be put.

Be specific. What outcome(s) will be accomplished using the desired funds, and how will these outcomes support institutional priorities? Why is the scale of the request appropriate (i.e., why is the specific amount being asked for, as opposed to a lesser or greater amount)? Why are you asking for funding at this particular time?

Be concise. Funding requests are not full reports; they should be written assuming an audience that is highly pressed for time. Every sentence should clearly support the specific request being made, and requests generally should not exceed 1–2 pages.

Articulate the stakes. If the funds are received, what will be the outcome? What good will be accomplished for the center, for students, and for the institution? If the funds are not received, what will be the outcome? What harm will be perpetrated (or, alternately, what good will fail to be accomplished) for the center, for students, and for the institution?

Ground requests in data. What evidence supports the urgent need for funding the programming/personnel/materials? What evidence supports success in attaining its intended goal of the programming/personnel/materials being funded? What evidence supports the center's effective past use of funding to effectively accomplish outcomes?

In making funding requests, it's always important to be patient. Funding approvals happen when requests are compelling and funds are available—it's more than possible for an excellent, well-articulated request to be denied simply because it's a challenging budget year, or more pressing concerns must be addressed. It may be necessary to submit a request several times (if possible, revising it based on feedback) before it is approved. Beginning with a pilot, using assessment data to show the effectiveness of a program, and requesting funding to scale up the program is always an effective strategy.

Institutional funds are not the only source of available funding. Grants from federal organizations, charitable foundations, and local organizations are all potential sources of funding for programming, infrastructure, technology, and other initiatives, and it is very likely that a department or individual on your campus can support you in finding potential grants that align with the center's priorities. Often, grants are used to create new programming that is then later "institutionalized" (permanently funded) by colleges/universities once it has proven itself and become an essential part of the student support system at the institution. Grants can be a highly effective long-term strategy, then, for attaining institutional funding.

Another highly effective way of speaking with administrators in a language that they understand is relaying the ways in which the center exemplifies best practices—approaches that have been broadly recognized within a scholarly and/or professional community as effective in achieving a desired goal, based on data-driven research—in higher education. Organizational leaders seek to create effective structures underneath them, and higher education as a field of knowledge unto itself has come to be deeply informed by research-based findings on what works in helping students to persist and succeed in college. Moreover, the highest-level administrators of colleges and universities are beholden to accrediting bodies, the organizations that certify institutions of higher education as meeting standards of excellence; much of higher education administration is organized around cycles of reaccreditation in which institutions demonstrate their ongoing fitness to receive funding and to grant credits and degrees that are viewed as externally valid. The criteria that accrediting bodies use to assess institutions are grounded in current best practices, which means that administrators are always looking for good examples of best practices taking places within the area of the institution that is their purview. In partnering with the administration, one effective tool is for LCAs to communicate ways in which their centers align with best practices for learning centers. Even more powerful, however, is to show ways in which the center aligns with overarching, broadly recognized best practices in higher education (e.g., the ways in which learning centers exemplify the characteristics of high-impact educational practices—see chapter 1). In doing so, LCAs simultaneously help administrators to accomplish their goals and highlight the roles their centers play as hubs for innovative, effective pedagogy and practices.

Finally, in cultivating a close relationship with the administration in which the center is resourced appropriately, it's important to be actively involved in current initiatives. Being a visible, active, and productive partner in large-scale projects that have their origin in major institutional goals and span multiple departments/units/divisions is a highly effective way to ensure that one's center is foremost in administrators' minds and to be broadly perceived as pertinent to the institution's future. Learning centers are logistically complex, and highly demanding of one's time and energy—it's easy to treat projects that fall outside of the internal demands of the center as peripheral. It's also easy to be skeptical of initiatives that an administration implements, viewing them as impositions on one's time, autonomy, and established way of doing things. Bringing energy and enthusiasm to such projects, however, whenever they can be generously construed as sanctioned by the center's mission, is an essential aspect of collaboration, not only with the administration but with the institution as a whole. When necessary, be proactive in asserting, via e-mails, personal communications, and other venues, the value of the learning center and of yourself as an LCA as a partner. Learning centers offer a highly effective model for increasing student expertise. They offer expertise on peer-led, collaborative, and active learning, as well as student leadership. They offer valuable insight into the student experience and a point of intersection with a wide cross-section of the student population. Learning centers are an invaluable partner in any student success initiative. When it's necessary to invite yourself to the table, do so—you belong there.

ADVISORY COUNCILS

Learning center advisory councils are one productive way of structuring collaborations while also involving center stakeholders in the work of the center. Learning center advisory councils meet on a regular basis (e.g., once a month, term, or academic year) to participate in activities such as reviewing assessment data, participating in strategic planning, responding to emerging issues, weighing in on center priorities, and generating ideas for programming.

Advisory councils should consist of representatives from major partner programs, as well as from each of the constituencies impacted by the center (student users, student employees, staff, faculty, administration). Learning center advisory councils may also include representatives from formal bodies such as faculty and student government. Advisory councils are a way to make sure that multiple perspectives are accounted for in the plans and activities of the center, as well as to benefit from the combined creativity of a large group of individuals in responding to challenges. Craig, Richardson, and Harris (2018) report the following common practices among learning centers in using advisory boards (pp. 99–100):

- Acting as a sounding board on learning center tactical/strategic planning
- Developing and supporting advocates for promoting the learning center
- Encouraging faculty involvement in the learning center
- Providing guidance for prioritizing learning center initiatives/services/budget requests
- Reviewing learning center status/data
- Ensuring that collaboration opportunities are maximized
- Providing specialized expertise to aid the learning center (e.g., statistical analysis, training)
- Providing student and faculty perspectives on services and marketing
- Promoting the services of the learning center
- Encouraging faculty participation in analyzing factors relevant to persistence and developing actions to promote permanence

Another benefit of advisory councils is that partners of the center come to appreciate, through dialogue, the priorities of other units and the needs for the center to be responsive to a variety of concerns. Finally, advisory councils are a powerful way to create widespread buy-in to the work of the center: individuals who have a stake in planning feel a greater sense of investment in seeing those plans come to fruition and are far more likely to act as ambassadors for the center in their other dealings on campus.

The categories listed here are only a few of the potential targets for collaboration, low-hanging fruit that every LCA should consider. Many others exist. Faculty development programs are potential partners in outreach to faculty; in programming that explores active, collaborative, and peer-led pedagogies in the classroom; and in the creation of a campus-wide conversation on excellence in learning. International studies units are possible collaborators in supporting the needs of English language learners. Residence life programs are potential allies in creating sites for peer tutoring that intersect in different ways with students' lives, making it easier for learners to access academic support. Every campus offers its own menu of possibilities, and it's essential to pursue them. Learning centers aren't just the beneficiaries of collaborations with other units; they are critically dependent on them. Learning centers exist at the heart of the academic experience and at the intersection of the many divisions that exist within every institution of higher education. It's imperative for LCAs to carefully form and grow collaborative relationships, so that a general goodwill toward the center is maintained, so that the center can serve as a hub for campus networks of academic support, and so that resources for supporting students as learners can be combined across organizational divisions.

QUESTIONS FOR PROGRAM ASSESSMENT

Collaborations with Academic Units

- Is regular communication for the purpose of sharing information and strategizing support maintained with all academic units with students who could potentially benefit from the services of the center?
- Do faculty in partner units have a clear understanding of the services that the center provides and the scenarios in which it would be appropriate to refer students to the center?
- Do faculty in partner units have a clear understanding of the needs, priorities, and values of the center with respect to student hiring, and are they leveraged as allies in seeking out potential candidates for positions as peer tutors?

Collaborations with Academic Advisors

- Do academic advisors have complete, up-to-date information on the services that the center provides and a robust understanding of how center services work?
- Do academic advisors understand the core pedagogy and target audience of the programs or services that comprise the center and understand the scenarios in which they might refer a student to different aspects of the center?
- Are advisors leveraged as a resource in developing programming that supports students' progress toward timely graduation?

Collaborations with Libraries

- Does the center maintain a collaboration with campus libraries that provides opportunities for programming collaboration, resource sharing, and mutual referrals?
- Does the center leverage librarians as resources on information literacy?

Collaborations with Student Resource Centers

• Does the student resource center leverage opportunities to engage in outreach to students who may not otherwise seek out the services of the center?
• Does the center leverage the expertise of staff in campus student resource centers on the unique needs of students they serve?
• Does the center leverage student resource centers as allies in creating a staff of peer tutors that reflects the diversity of the student body?

Collaborations with Accessibility Resource Centers

• Is the accessibility resource center leveraged as a source of advice and guidance in attending to the needs of neurodiverse learners?
• Is the accessibility resource center leveraged as a source of insight on accessibility, ensuring that all aspects of the center are fully accessible for students with disabilities?
• Is the accessibility resource center leveraged as a source of insight on universal design, ensuring that the physical and virtual presence of the center is designed in a way that makes the needs of physically and cognitively diverse learners a central concern?
• Is the accessibility resource center leveraged as a source of insight on technologies, pedagogical approaches, and ethical concerns that tutors should be attentive to in sessions with physically and cognitively diverse learners?
• Does the accessibility resource center have detailed, up-to-date information on learning center services that are particularly pertinent to the needs of physically and cognitively diverse learners?

Collaborations with Centers for Counseling and Mental Health

• Do tutors have clear guidance, informed by the centers for counseling and mental health, on scenarios in which they should notify a supervisor and/or refer students to the services of the center for counseling and mental health?
• Is the center for counseling and mental health leveraged as a source of insight on attending to students' affective states in tutoring sessions and/or as a programming partner that attends to learners as emotional beings?

Collaborations with Other Learning Centers on Campus

• Does the center work (if relevant) with other learning centers on campus to ensure that students have access to seamless and comprehensive academic support?

- Does the center collaborate (if relevant) with other campus learning centers to work together toward shared goals, with each center contributing according to its areas of specialization and expertise?
- Does the center work to ensure that LCAs and peer tutors within each individual learning center have a full understanding of the services that the other provides so that all parties can think collaboratively about ways of working together to ensure that every student on campus has access to robust academic support?
- Does the center work to ensure that all students on campus clearly understand their reasons for choosing one center over another in specific scenarios and have a clear idea of how to access peer tutoring?

Collaboration with Administration

- Does the administration have a clear idea of the mission, methods, and services of the center, including ways that the center uses recognized best practices in supporting student success?
- Are assessment and reporting practices in place that provide the administration with regular information on the center's impact in supporting institutional priorities?
- Is the center involved as a visible, active, and productive partner in current, large-scale institutional initiatives that support administrative priorities?

Chapter Eight

Advertising and Marketing

Peer tutoring is a model with enormous potential for effecting change both for individual students and for campus-wide cultures of learning, and every campus is full of students who stand to benefit from the services that learning centers offer:

- An enhanced understanding of course concepts
- Mentorship in disciplinary modes of writing, thinking, and problem solving
- A deeper awareness of themselves as learners
- Greater awareness of strategies that successful students apply for learning and for life

Despite the potential benefits, students might have any number of reasons not to take advantage of peer tutoring. They may find it to be a counterproductive use of their time, the potential benefits outweighed by the inconvenience or lost time. They may feel that tutoring is only relevant for a type of student (less senior, less capable, less well-prepared) that they are not, or that by taking advantage of peer tutoring they identify themselves as unintelligent. They may feel that the center is intimidating, full of overachievers with whom they do not identify or outspoken students with whom they do not want to compete for attention. They may not understand how center services work and wish to avoid showing up without knowing what to do. They may feel embarrassed by their own lack of knowledge or preparation. They may be simply unaware that the center offers services that are relevant to them or even that the center exists.

STUDENT PERCEPTIONS OF ACADEMIC SUPPORT

A number of studies from the literature on academic support have inquired into the ways that students' perception of peer tutoring can function as barriers for learners in seeking out support from which they would likely benefit:

- Bannier (2007), reporting the results of a study examining college students' use of mathematics tutoring in a learning center, indicated that students may not perceive the services of the center as relevant to them if they have a relatively high level of confidence in the relevant area of study.
- Goldstein, Sauer, and O'Donnell (2014), based on a study of factors impacting students' use of supplemental instruction in an introductory accounting course, report that students are less likely to use support if they have a negative impression of the service or believe that it won't help them in meeting their academic goals.
- Cheatle and Bullerjahn (2015) found that a widespread belief that the services of the university writing center are relevant only to first-year students was a factor in creating lower usage among upper-division students.

Beliefs about peer tutoring can be intensely local, shaped by the institution's history, by the home cultures represented among the student body, and by learners' individual pre-college experiences with peer tutoring. Understanding the negative narratives about the center that exist on campus (through surveys, focus groups, or simply talking to students) and where they may cluster in academic programs, majors, or class years is a necessary first step in changing those narratives. These ideas can be replaced with more beneficial attitudes toward the learning center through sustained marketing and outreach efforts.

One important function of advertising and marketing is to give students and other stakeholders information on what the center is, the nature of the services it offers, and how to access them. To just as great an extent, the purpose of advertising and marketing is to create a narrative around the learning center that counteracts negative attitudes that students may have about peer tutoring and that makes it likelier for students to use it:

- The center is a cool, relaxed, intellectually engaging place.
- All types of students can be found there.
- It's open to and helpful for students at all levels of achievement and all levels of progress in their academic journey.
- The center is a student-led, student-driven space.
- It's a normal, everyday part of student life on campus.
- Successful students are successful precisely because they take advantage of peer tutoring.

The feelings, attitudes, and emotions evoked in individuals in connection to the center together comprise the center's brand. Every center has a brand: a way it is widely thought of by students, faculty, and other stakeholders. The extent to which this brand aligns with the center's mission—and with the ways that LCAs hope for their centers to be perceived on their campuses—is determined by preconceptions about tutoring, by past experiences with the center, and by a variety of other factors. Through marketing and outreach, LCAs have the incredible ability to shape the center's brand, crafting and broadcasting a coherent message about what the center is, who it's for, its relevance, and how stakeholders should feel about it. LCAs have a number of powerful tools at their disposal to do so.

PRINTED MATERIALS

Printed materials may include brochures, bookmarks, handouts, flyers, or other tangible, ink-on-paper instruments of outreach. Delivered to faculty mailboxes, handed out to students in class visits, stocked in information kiosks around campus, distributed to academic advisors, providing off-hours information for learners at the front desk of the center, circulated at orientation events, and otherwise disseminated, printed materials play the role of saturating the campus with both easy-to-access information on the center and spreading awareness of the services that it provides.

Through printed materials, learning centers cast a wide net, and inevitably, a high proportion of publications will end up unread or discarded. But this widespread dissemination creates as many opportunities as possible for the right documents to reach the right readers at the right time, providing the push that they need in order to take advantage of the services of the center. For students, printed materials often act as a physical token for a referral to the center: a brochure or bookmark that an instructor or advisor hands them is both a tangible reminder of the referral and a guide on how to take advantage of it. For faculty, advisors, and other partners, publications can empower them to advocate for the center in referring learners who could benefit from its services, providing them with the information that they need to make informed referrals grounded in an accurate understanding of the center, its pedagogies, and its services. All of the printed materials that the center creates should be crafted with the needs of a specific target audience in mind, designed with mindfulness of the concerns of that audience and how the services that the center provides address those concerns.

The cost of printed materials can be significant, and it's important for a center of any size to be strategic in the development and distribution of printed materials. Items with a higher printing cost (e.g., materials in color, those with a glossy finish, or printed on high-quality paper/cardstock) are often

CAMPUS COMMUNICATIONS OFFICES
AS MARKETING PARTNERS

On many campuses, a central office attends to marketing and communications for the institution as a whole, creating a cohesive brand for the college/university and advancing it through recruitment publications, the institutional website, official social media accounts, and other channels (usually, this office is also charged with internal messaging, ensuring that all campus units follow branding practices that support the overall marketing efforts of the institution). This office, and the individuals within it, represent an incredible resource for LCAs. Marketing, design, social media, and Web design are all highly specialized fields of knowledge; the difference between what a competent novice and a skilled professional can create is vast, and the gap is immediately apparent to audiences. The professionals in communications offices are often available to consult on the design of logos, printed materials, and websites, as well as on the approach and tone of social media campaigns. In some cases, they may be available as partners in the creation of marketing materials or even entire marketing campaigns.

Communications offices also make good partners in creating a widespread awareness of the center. Communications offices are in the business of creating materials that cast the institution in a positive light. The types of interactions that take place every day in learning centers—students helping students, using active, collaborative, and innovative pedagogies—make for powerful, compelling images and stories in official institutional outreach channels. Consider pitching ideas for content from the center to the campus communications office, or inviting the campus photographer to focus their lens on the work of the center (making sure, of course, that all students photographed provide permission before their image is used in any promotional materials). Content from the center, broadcasted through the official institution-wide channels that communications offices maintain, can significantly boost the campus profile of the center while also supporting the goal of the communications office to showcase excellence within the institution.

reserved for higher-stakes, lower-distribution applications such as brochures and public reports (although some situations call for creating a large number of high-quality publications—the launch of a new center, for example, or of a significant programming initiative). It's also wise, in more costly publications, to minimize information that is liable to change on a term-to-term basis (e.g., hours for specific subjects), reducing the possibility of holding a large reserve of costly documents that contain outdated information.

Lower-cost materials (e.g., smaller items using sparse color, printed on lower-quality paper or rendered in a matte finish) are generally best used in situations when distribution is large and information is ephemeral (e.g., a half-sheet advertising an upcoming event, or providing current hours and services for a particular subject area). Many centers develop a signature form of publication for widespread distribution to students (e.g., at new-student orientations or in class visits) that strikes a middle path between these two extremes. Often a bookmark or postcard-size item, containing a few key pieces of information on the services of the center and how to use them, aspires to be both small enough to be inexpensive to print in large numbers and strong enough to survive at the bottom of a student's backpack until needed.

In all applications, regardless of cost, effective design is essential. Printed materials are a critical vehicle for creating a campus-wide awareness of the center and its identity. The visual language (colors, fonts, imagery, logos, etc.) used in them should be consistent across all publications, demonstrating a coherent, carefully crafted brand. Clear, reader-oriented prose that explains the services of the center in a way that will resonate for learners (as opposed to language rooted in the academic and professional communities of learning centers, which may present as opaque to readers from outside that community) is essential. So, too, is imagery that conveys the way the LCA wishes the center to be perceived by its stakeholders. In all regards, the printed materials that represent the center to its stakeholders should convey not only clarity and professionalism, but also the values that motivate the center's work.

CENTER PUBLICATIONS

Jackson and Grutsch McKinney (2012) report the results of a survey of 141 writing centers, seeking to shed light on emerging identities for writing centers and on the ways that writing center directors spend their time. Responses to their question on the types of publications that the center creates provide both an interesting cross-section of how LCAs strategize outreach and a helpful catalog of potential means of marketing (adapted from Jackson & Grutsch McKinney, 2012, p. 6):

Type of Publication	Respondents
Website	102 (72%)
Brochures	96 (68%)
Bookmark, Stickers	78 (55%)
Reports	78 (55%)
Posters	60 (42%)
T-shirts, Pens, Pencils, Mugs, Promotional Items	48 (34%)
Bulletin Board	47 (33%)
Newsletter	33 (23%)
Video, Slidecast	22 (16%)
Blog	11 (8%)
Podcast	10 (7%)
Newspaper Column, Articles	8 (6%)
Other	20 (14%)
Total offering at least one publication	132 (94%)

ONLINE MARKETING

Marketing through digital forums and online communities offers the opportunity to reach a large audience at little cost, making it possible to create a widespread awareness of the central messaging of the center among not only students, but other groups of stakeholders as well (e.g., faculty, staff members, parents). Online marketing makes it possible to interact with one's audience in ways that simply aren't possible through other forms of outreach, fostering an active engagement with the community that the center serves. And it has an immediacy that makes it well-suited to responding to the current moment, rapidly distributing messaging that is responsive to learners' immediate needs.

WEB DESIGN FOR LEARNING CENTERS

The most important audience to consider for any learning center in creating a Web presence is students, who will generally use the center's site in order to access (or get information on accessing) academic support. Honoring a few core principles will help make doing so a good experience for learners while also maximizing the site's potential as a tool for outreach.

Less Is More

The more words on a page, the less likely they are to be read. Large blocks of prose are off-putting for students (and for Web audiences more generally). Similarly, navigation options should be constrained as much as possible. The goal is not to document every aspect of the center, but to create a clean, straightforward experience for users.

Make Learner Needs the Organizing Principle

Students—the primary audience of a learning center's website—won't generally visit your site in order to gain an overarching picture of the center and its programming. They'll visit in order to get information on how to address their current need (e.g., getting support for a sociology paper they need to write or an economics exam taking place the next day). Design your center's site around facilitating students' access to information on how to access the services of the center, not your center's hierarchical organization.

Use Images to Convey Vital Information about the Center

Images are key in Web design. Although vanishingly few site visitors will seek out your mission statement, or read through descriptions of your programming and motivating values, every single individual who accesses your site will see the pictures that you use as header images. The human mind is remarkably rapid and astute at drawing information from images. Pictures should be carefully curated (ideally selected from high-quality images of learning interactions in the center) to convey important implicit information on what to expect in sessions, how tutoring works, who the tutors are, and what the center is like.

Make Accessibility a Central Concern

Usability for learners exemplifying the full spectrum of physical and neural diversity is essential for learning centers and mandatory for learning center websites. Ensure that navigation is straightforward, that text is easily visible (and appears in a form that can be read by transcription software), and that all aspects of the site behave in predictable and transparent ways. The World Wide Web Content Accessibility Guidelines (Chisholm, Vanderheiden, & Jacobs, 2001) provide a full set of guidelines commonly used in higher education as a standard for Web accessibility and form an excellent set of recommendations for learning centers in attending to the needs of diverse learners in creating a Web presence.

Consider Mobile Users First

The overwhelming majority of students will access your center's site from a phone or other mobile device. Their experience, not of those who visit the site on a desktop computer or laptop, should be of primary concern. In considering structure, verbiage, images, and all other aspects of the design, make decisions based on the majority of users who will view the site on a small screen navigated using touch, rather than the minority who will view it on a large screen, navigating it with a mouse and keyboard.

The most essential and widespread form of online marketing for learning centers is through a website. A learning center's website is, in many ways, the online correlate to the physical space of the center. Certainly, this is the case in the way that it serves as a point of entry to and repository for the programs and services contained within the center. Learning center websites serve as the primary location for current, accurate information on hours, locations, programming, and other vital information for students on how to access services. Frequently, it is also a venue for students to make appointments (through an interface with the learning center management software, or through a live chat function that can also serve as a forum for asking questions). In centers that have online resources and/or tutoring services, the site will also serve as a portal to these services. In the same way that the entrance to a learning center plays a critical function in the design of the physical space of learning center (see chapter 6), the home page (the page advertised in all outreach, which serves as the starting for navigation to all other pages) is vital in creating a positive experience for users. The home page should clearly signal the overall organization of the site and make clear the path to the information, resources, and services that are contained within it.

Even more important, however, a learning center's website fulfills the same function as the physical space of the center in shaping how the center exists in the minds of its users and other stakeholders. It's essential for a center's website to convey an identity that aligns with the mission of the center and to invite learners into the space in the same way that the center's physical entrance does. For many students, a visit to the center's website isn't just a low-stakes, convenient way to get information on using the center's services. It's an inquiry into what the center is, how it's relevant to them, and whether using it can align with their sense of identity as a student. No function is more important for a learning center's website than to be inviting for learners and to present the image of the center that the LCA wishes to project to students and other potential audiences (faculty, academic staff, the administration, parents, and others).

CULTIVATING AN EFFECTIVE SOCIAL MEDIA PRESENCE

Learning center outreach through social media introduces the formidable challenge of competing for likes, shares, and attention with the wide array of actors vying for young adults' attention in digital spaces. In order to compete in the crowded online spaces of the major social media channels, it's essential to create content that grabs students' attention and aligns with their interests.

- **Avoid depending on social media as a place to convey vital information.** The lowest hanging fruit in using social media for marketing is to use it as a means to broadcast center programming, hours, and policies. Unfortunately, doing so is a rather ineffective use of social media. In order to create an effective social media presence, it's far more important for an LCA to consider what appeals to college students and the impression of the center the viewer will get than to convey any particular set of facts or information about the center.
- **Make first impressions your first priority.** People don't scroll carefully and thoroughly through their social media feeds; they scroll through them in stolen moments. If a post is to be absorbed, it must be interesting and appealing in the half-glance that a social media user devotes to a post in the

moment of deciding whether to give it a few seconds of their full attention. The most effective social media content is short, digestible, and entertaining. Images, videos, and events create much higher levels of interest than information, prose, or announcements.

- **Focus on creating engagement.** The goal of posting through social media isn't to broadcast information but to create engagement (often, this will take the form of liking, sharing, or commenting). Think of your social media channels as two-way communication, and consider ways that you can invite your audience to interact with your posts.
- **Be active in the comments.** The original post is one opportunity to engage with your audience; comments are another. After your post, being active in the comments is a great way to demonstrate engagement and be attentive to concerns, as well as to make sure that inappropriate comments are flagged for removal.
- **Build a following.** Great posts don't matter if no one sees them! Cultivate a following by encouraging students to follow the center's social media feeds in presentations and workshops, doing giveaways to followers, asking other campus programs with a successful social media presence to repost items from your feed, and otherwise working to build an audience for your social media presence.
- **Carefully consider which platform(s) you use to create a presence.** YouTube, Facebook, Instagram, and SnapChat were, as of 2019, the most commonly used among 18–24-years-olds (Pew Research Center, 2019b). Each of them offers a very different set of tools and is used for different reasons; the LCA should carefully consider their goals in selecting a platform (or platforms) through which to create a presence.
- **Be prolific and be consistent.** Occasional, sporadic posts don't count for much in the world of social media. In order to register with users (and in some cases, even to appear in their feeds), it's important to create a large, evenly distributed amount of content. Remember that posts don't have to take a lot of time to create. A series of videos on learning strategies, released on a weekly basis, is great content. So, however, are pictures of learning interactions in the center, or study tips from tutors, posted throughout the day.
- **Leverage student employees as a resource.** Learning centers have an incredible asset in peer tutors, representatives of the center who have deep, firsthand knowledge of how college students use social media and what constitutes "good" content on each platform. Use them as sample audiences for posts, creators of content for your feeds, and advisors on what students look for in social media presence from campus organizations. At a higher level of responsibility, individual students can even take a leadership role in coordinating the center's social media on a specific platform and responding to users' comments to posts.

A more dynamic, interactive form of outreach is available through social media. Social media use has rapidly become deeply ingrained in our society, nowhere more so than among college-age students who have come of age in the years since social media has come to effect sweeping changes in the landscapes of media, communication, the professional world, and education alike. According to a 2019 report on social media use from the Pew Research Center (2019a), 90% of 18–29-year-olds make regular use of at least one social media platform (up from 7% in 2005).

Perhaps even more striking than this figure is the amount of time that college students spend on social media. The Cooperative Institutional Research Program at the Higher Education Research Institute at UCLA (2018) reports that 59.6% of college freshmen spend more than 5 hours/week on social media, 32.3% spend more than 10, 19.4% spend more than 15, and 11.5% spend more than 20. Outreach through social media represents an unparalleled opportunity for learning centers to reach students in the (digital) spaces where they spend their time, as well as to reach other groups of stakeholders in older age groups who also regularly use at least one social media platform (82% of 30–49-year-olds, 69% of 50–64-year-olds, and 40% of those 65 years or older, according to the same 2019 Pew report).

As a marketing tool, the goal in establishing a social media presence is to cultivate an awareness and impression of the center that, hopefully, for some portion of viewers, will result in their ultimately becoming clients or advocates of the center—an incredible opportunity, as the widespread use of social media among students makes it possible to reach individuals and populations with whom it may be otherwise challenging to make contact. As an outreach tool, however, the potential is even larger: through social media, it's possible for a learning center to have an impact on campus that far exceeds the direct, student-to-student contact that it facilitates. Posts that show the value of active approaches to learning, that normalize the use of academic support resources, that foster students' awareness of their processes for learning, that encourage students to share insight with one another, and that educate learners on the strategies that successful students use all advance the highest-level outcomes of the center even if the students impacted never set foot in the center.

As an educational venue, social media has significant constraints—the same can be said, however, for any learning forum. The limitations of social media as a forum for learning also represent unique opportunities: for example, Trowbridge, Waterbury, and Sudbury (2017) describe the potential for social media to facilitate microlearning—short, focused, potentially highly impactful bursts of learning—while also deepening learning, creating learning communities, and increasing student engagement. The limited amount of time and attention that viewers may be willing to devote to any one particular post notwithstanding, learning centers can leverage their social media presence to make meaningful, positive changes to the very culture of learning that exists on campus.

INVOLVING STUDENTS IN MARKETING

Breslin et al. (2018), arguing to include peer tutors in higher-order aspects of learning center administration, take note of marketing and outreach as areas where centers can benefit significantly from the deep involvement of peer tutors and encourage LCAs to "leverage peer educators' tacit knowledge of their own preferences, their peer groups, and the institution's particular student culture, to assist with the conceptualization and strategic planning of promotion and outreach" (p. 56). Similarly, Truman (2019), in articulating the value in involving tutors in creating social media content, notes that partnering with peer educators in center outreach is an enormous asset in creating a branding strategy to meet students where they are. You have many possible ways to involve peer tutors in your center's marketing strategy, taking advantage of their unique status as both students and employees while also increasing their engagement and helping them to build a professional portfolio. We include a few ideas here; peer tutors are the best source for more possibilities. Consider having tutors

- provide student feedback on the center's existing marketing materials, suggesting ways of making them more appealing for students.
- participate in a contest to develop a logo or slogan to be used as a centerpiece in the marketing efforts for the center (or for a program within the center).
- create flyers or posters for the center to be printed and posted around campus.
- find daily quotes on learning to put in a prominent space in the center.
- write pieces on their work with learners or the learning strategies they apply in their own studies, or interesting ideas from their disciplines, for a center newsletter/blog.
- develop posts for social media accounts.
- take pictures of great learning interactions in the center for use in marketing materials.
- create chalk art around campus advertising center events.
- serve as focus groups regarding how to reach students in their majors, teams, clubs, and so forth.
- decorate the entrance to the center with inviting, seasonally appropriate imagery.
- develop their own marketing ideas, based on their knowledge of students in their programs (and perhaps even on their developing expertise in marketing, business, graphic design, digital communication, rhetoric, or other relevant areas of the curriculum).

E-mail, that oldest and most straightforward form of digital communication, should in no way be underestimated as a form of outreach: checking one's e-mail regularly is nearly a prerequisite for modern life, making e-mail a powerful tool for distributing information quickly and widely. Outreach by e-mail should take into account the major limitation of the medium: everyone gets a lot of it, and many e-mails are deleted or marked as read without being opened. This makes it important to communicate vital information in subject lines (e.g., "The Learning Center opens for the Fall on Monday!"; "Midterm Review for Chem 101 this Friday at 3 in the SUB"). Also, ensure that e-mails are targeted, containing information specifically relevant to recipients: listservs of faculty, staff, and students (as well as more specific groups of students, such as first-years or international students) are maintained on many campuses, making it possible to distribute customized messages that address the needs of specific groups.

Finally, whereas with social media it's important to communicate often, with e-mail it's more important to communicate impactfully. Senders perceived as cluttering up recipients' inboxes with numerous, irrelevant messages may be filtered, either informally (scanned but never opened) or formally (blocked or unsubscribed). E-mail communications should provide recipients with information that is helpful, relevant, and timely (e.g., to announce the beginning of services for the term to students, to announce an important change in programming to advisors, or to distribute suggested syllabus language on the learning center to faculty). Many centers also use e-mail to disseminate a periodical electronic newsletter/blog or set of announcements and updates, which consolidate what might otherwise be annoyingly frequent e-mail communications to a reassuringly regular rhythm of pertinent communications from the center.

EVENTS AS MARKETING

A learning center that functions well is always engaging in meaningful, effective programming that is highly relevant to the needs of students on the campus it serves. The ongoing nature of the work can, in some ways, make it challenging to market: in advertising, consistent, unchanging messages are tuned out by audiences over time. Learning center events (e.g., workshops, reviews, study groups, or "pop-up" tutoring events at offsite locations) allow peer tutoring pedagogy to be delivered in a specialized, unique way. At the same time, they provide an opportunity to market the center in ways that rise above the background noise of the information bombarding students, fostering a deeper awareness of the center's mission. When a learning center creates a marketing push around an event (e.g., by posting it as an event on social media, sending e-mail announcements, and distributing flyers around campus), it does far more than just increase attendance at the event. It creates a widespread awareness of the center itself and the type of academic support it offers.

Take the example of marketing around a learning center workshop on the topic of note taking: only a small portion of students who see advertising for the event may attend, but every viewer will, to some extent, internalize the fact that the learning center exists and it supports note taking. Similarly, when an event is marketed to a specific group or course, the group targeted (again, whether or not they attend) becomes aware that the center is attentive to their needs and has relevant programming for them. Events represent an opportunity for LCAs to create not only a broader awareness of the center, but a more accurate, fine-grained knowledge of what the center is and what it does.

FACE-TO-FACE OUTREACH

Face-to-face outreach, in the most literal sense, meets learners where they are. By being proactive in bringing the center to students rather than passively waiting for students to come to the center, LCAs can effectively lower the barriers that stand between students and use of academic support. Student groups and off-site locations replace learners' negative attitudes toward and misperceptions of peer tutoring with accurate, grounded impressions of the center and how they stand to benefit from it.

Visits to classes are a simple, powerful outreach tool that takes the best possible advantage of the center's greatest asset: peer tutors. In class visits, peer tutors visit courses that the center supports to introduce themselves, describe the center's services that are relevant to students in the class, and field questions about the center. In meeting and engaging with tutors, students' fears about tutors and tutoring are replaced with the reality that tutors are cool, interesting, unintimidating, approachable, relatable individuals; students like themselves who have butted heads with the challenges of the course they are currently enrolled in and have helpful lessons to impart from the experience.

At the same time, tutors plant a seed for growing a relationship with the instructor of the course, establishing a channel of communication supporting further collaboration. Class visits are most effective either at the beginning of the term (when tutors are trained and working scheduled shifts but not yet busy) or in moments when major assessments such as exams, projects, and papers are approaching (when students are particularly receptive to information on resources that will help them accomplish their goals).

They have the most impact in large, introductory courses, where they will affect the greatest number of learners for the greatest portion of their college experience. Generally, the tutor most relevant to the course in question should visit the class (e.g., a Spanish tutor will visit Spanish 101). It's critical, however, that tutors visiting a course act not only as representatives of the program/service they provide, but of the center as a whole, speaking to all of the programs within the center that are relevant to the course (e.g., an SI leader visiting biology 101 on behalf of the center might speak not only to supplemental instruction, but also, as relevant, to individual appointments, drop-in labs, online tutoring, learning strategies support, and writing support).

In larger centers, class visits are best centrally coordinated by LCAs or senior tutors who can manage outreach to faculty to request permission to visit courses and assign visits to individual tutors, avoid duplication of efforts, and ensure that every visit is known by the center, expected by faculty, and compensated for tutors. Peer tutors should always have the opportunity to plan class visits in advance—it's extremely important to provide tutors with clear guidance for what to cover in class visits, and an opportunity to practice delivering their talk in advance of the visit. (*The Rowman & Littlefield Guide for Peer Tutors* [Sanford 2020] offers a full framework and set of talking points for class visits.)

The critical information for tutors to deliver in class visits is the contact information for the center; how to access the center's services, all of the center's services that are relevant for students in the course, and scenarios in which (based on the tutor's specific, fine-grained knowledge of the particular course they are visiting) it might be beneficial for learners to seek the services of a peer tutor. Along the way, it's helpful for tutors to communicate the facts that, first, they were once a student in the course they are visiting, and are able to offer hard-won insight into how to succeed in it; and, second, that it's not necessary to prepare for a tutoring appointment, but rather that learners should come as they are, at whatever point they are in the learning process. Visits to clubs, teams, organizations, and other student affiliation groups can play out similarly, with tutors focusing on the way that specific services that the center provides are of particular relevance to students in the group. Such visits are most effective when the tutor who visits a group is affiliated with it and is able to use that affiliation both to arrange the visit and to speak to the particular needs of the group (e.g., a tutor who is also a student athlete might coordinate with a coach to arrange a visit to a team's study hall, where he can relate to fellow athletes over their busy schedules and travel calendars and recommend the center's support for time management and online tutoring).

GIVEAWAY ITEMS

A common practice for learning centers is to distribute inexpensive giveaway items (swag) bearing the center's branding to students at orientations, class visits, and other events. Such items can include clothing (e.g., hats and T-shirts) but more commonly comprises small, useful objects that have been printed with the center's core marketing information (e.g., the center's name, logo, slogan, and Web address). The ideal bit of swag is an object useful enough to college students (e.g., a pen, a pencil, a notebook, a water bottle, etc.) that they will carry in their everyday life, ideally reminding them of the center in a moment when its services would be helpful to them and seen every day by other students. Another common giveaway item for is planners, which send the implicit messages that time management is important, as well as that it is within the purview of the center. For centers able to make the not-inconsiderable financial investment required to purchase a large enough collection of items that they can be distributed to a meaningful portion of the student population, swag can be highly effective in creating widespread awareness of the center.

Orientation events are critical sites for face-to-face outreach. It's important and reassuring for students to receive information on relevant academic support programming as they enter the institution and/or specific majors or programs within it. For this reason, it's essential that LCAs cultivate relationships with administrators of orientation programs—most particularly, of new student orientation—that provide them with access. But orientation events represent a unique set of challenges. Students in orientations are bombarded with volumes of information on every aspect of college life at a moment when they are undergoing an intense emotional experience.

Consider the goal of your presentation at an orientation event. If it is to have students retain detailed information on the center's services and how to access them, your goal is nearly hopeless. If, however, it is for students to retain an impression of the learning center as a welcoming, helpful space relevant to them, then your goal is more attainable.

Ideally, orientation sessions should focus on the attendees' current life transition and model the type of support they can expect to receive through the center (e.g., at a new student orientation event, presenters might engage with attendees—through as active and collaborative a session as the format allows—over the challenges of the transition from high school to college, and discuss strategies for studying, learning, and time management). The center's core message should be that the center is a normal, everyday part of the student experience, and using it is a habit that defines successful students.

As much as possible, orientation programming should involve tutors. The logistics of orientation events, often taking place at a point in the term when tutors are not yet scheduled and involving audience sizes that can be daunting for students, can make this challenging. Involving tutors as co-presenters or as facilitators of breakout sessions are good ways to involve tutors if they are willing and able to attend; prominently invoking the tutors in other ways is essential if they are not (e.g., showing new first-year students a slide of the advice that peer tutors would give themselves if they could go back in time and speak to themselves at new-student orientation). As in all face-to-face outreach, it's far more important for learners to have a positive impression of the tutors than it is for them to internalize any particular piece of information.

No one approach to marketing is so effective that it makes others unnecessary. Nor can face-to-face, print, and digital approaches be meaningfully ranked in order of their relative importance to the center's overarching outreach efforts. Each approach and each specific tool (as well as other outreach opportunities, unique to specific institutional contexts) takes advantage of different channels, offers different advantages, and reaches different audiences. What is important is to create an outreach plan that combines multiple methods in order to convey a clear, consistent message to the campus community and sets as its goal to ensure that every individual who stands to benefit from the services of the center understands the relevance of the center to their personal goals.

QUESTIONS FOR PROGRAM ASSESSMENT

Overall Marketing Approach

- Does the center communicate, through its marketing efforts, a view of the center that actively counteracts negative perceptions that students may have of tutoring and academic support?
- Does the center communicate, through its marketing efforts, a clear and consistent brand and set of values?
- Does the center use a wide variety of outreach methods to create a concerted approach to marketing that reaches stakeholders in multiple ways and takes advantage of the complementary strengths of printed, online, and face-to-face approaches?

Printed Materials

- Does the center use a variety of printed publications, each crafted for a different audience, to create widespread awareness of the center and its services on campus?

- Does the center communicate, through its marketing efforts, a clear and consistent brand?
- Do printed materials have an attractive, professional design?
- Are publications written with a strong awareness of the needs and preferences of the intended audience, conveying the messaging of the center in a way that is relevant and appealing for readers?

Online Marketing

- Does the center have and maintain a website that contains clear information on how to access the center's services, is a portal for all online services and resources that the center offers, is welcoming and accessible for all users, and conveys the center's values?
- Does the center take advantage of a variety of social media platforms currently popular among students to create an interesting, appealing, engaging social media presence, posting frequently and strategically to create widespread awareness of the center's brand and make positive changes to the culture of learning on campus?
- Does the center use regular, periodic e-mail messages to target audiences to distribute important, relevant, and timely information about the center?

Face-to-Face Outreach

- Does the center use face-to-face outreach to create a clear, grounded impression of the center and peer tutors?
- Do peer tutors visit courses they support to introduce themselves, convey the center's core messaging, and distribute information on how to use its services?
- Does the center have a role in key orientation events, and use it to model the center's approaches, provide students with a positive impression of the center, and convey the relevance of the center to their current life transition?

Chapter Nine

Reporting and Assessment

Learning center assessment has two goals.

The first is internal. Within the center, assessment periodically and systematically checks the extent to which a program is effectively fulfilling its mission and goals. Assessment gathers data from all available sources to objectively ascertain the effect that its services have on the student population that it serves, actively seeking out those areas in which the center could make improvements to have as much impact as possible. Assessment drives change and decision making within the center, drawing an LCA's attention to those areas that are models that can be touted and used as a springboard for further development, and to those areas of programming that may need attention or reorganization, or simply may not be fulfilling their intention and should be eliminated. Assessment drives funding and resourcing decisions, highlighting those areas of the center that most deserve funds, space, and personnel hours, that are not effectively using allocated resources, or that are being hindered by a lack of resources. Assessment drives planning, determining where professional staff efforts should be directed in moving the program steadily, year-by-year, toward the greatest possible degree of programmatic excellence and effect on the student population it serves.

Assessment also has an external goal. Assessment is the basis for articulating, to campus stakeholders, the value that the center adds to the institution. For students and faculty, reporting based on assessment data can demonstrate the impact of center services, inviting visits to, collaboration with, and investment in a center that is widely viewed—based on clear reporting of robust data—as an effective, impactful service. For college and university administrators, assessment data illustrate the effectiveness of peer tutoring and of the learning center model, attesting to the role that the center plays in supporting the larger mission of the institution and to the powerful way that learning centers can convert institutional investment of funding, space, and personnel into real, measurable gains in student success.

UTILIZATION DATA

Utilization data—basic information gleaned as students log in and out of center services, compiled over a period of time—are the most basic and fundamental measure at an LCA's disposal for understanding patterns of use within the center. Typical and profoundly helpful measures of center utilization include (for any given span of time) the total number of students served, total visits of student users, the total contact hours with student users, and the average number of visits per student user. Each of these measures can be applied to a center overall or to individual programs within it, and by academic year or term (or any other unit of time). Utilization data are capable of telling a powerful, effective, and succinct story about a center's reach and impact, and providing an at-a-glance measure of the work accomplished by and for students within the center.

COLLECTING DATA ON STUDENT UTILIZATION

The first step (and absolutely necessary prerequisite) in assessment and reporting is collecting accurate data on learners' visits to the center.

- Provide a single point of entry and exit to the center, through which students must pass in order to enter or exit the center. If you have alternate paths of access and egress, students can and will use them instead of waiting to log in and out.
- Capture both the time that students log in to the center and the time they log out. This provides valuable information on how long students stay in the center and makes it possible to calculate overall student contact hours.
- Make logging in and out completely consistent. A student user who has learned that it's not strictly necessary to log in every time (or, alternately a student employee who has learned that it's acceptable to let some students through without doing so) is very unlikely to make it a habit.
- In drop-in tutoring formats, appoint a tutor or other student worker to the dedicated role of logging students in and out of the center. Student workers who juggle the competing obligations of tutoring and attending to student intake will generally focus on the former to the detriment of the latter.
- In individual appointments and group learning scenarios, it's possible to have tutors record information on sessions using logs or sign-in sheets. Be sure to include robust training on logging students in and out, and to make

it an explicit, enforced aspect of employment to collect and turn in accurate reports daily.

- At log-in, collect needed information on who students are (e.g., their major) and what they are doing in the center (e.g., meeting with a writing tutor), as well as the class for which they are seeking support. This should be balanced with the need to make logging in fast and easy, a process that shouldn't take more than a few seconds.
- Use a software system that makes logging students in and out simple and automatic. Any of the popular tutoring scheduling software platforms (see chapter 3, text box 1) have this function. It's possible to create local software platforms or make creative use of tools such as online forms or spreadsheets. Be aware, however, that these tools may lack the ease of use—as well as the ability to export information in reports—that purpose-built systems allow.
- Make gathering student ID numbers part of your process for logging in and out, or make sure they are attached to the accounts that students create. Collecting these unique student IDs is essential to correlating user information to institutional data on academics and demographic background.
- If possible, have students log in and out by swiping their student ID cards (a feature of most of the common tutor scheduling platforms). This makes logging in much faster and makes for far more accurate tracking—students mistyping their ID number is a very significant source of inaccurate data. Consider your campus's office for information technology as a resource; it may be able to offer either support or the use of a larger campus-wide system.

Combined with demographic and student data, utilization data can provide further insight into the students who use the center. Information on the programs and majors represented among the users speaks to the areas of the curriculum that the center currently serves; information on academic rank and standing can provide insight into the types of students who are, and are not, seeking the center's services (e.g., first-year students? Students with strong GPAs? Students with low entrance-exam scores?). Data on gender, nationality, race, language background, and other aspects of student identity can provide a clear picture of who makes use of the center and how this group may differ in composition from the student body at large. Most pointedly, these data can speak to the center's possible impact on at-risk student populations such as first-generation college students, Pell-eligible students, students from underrepresented minorities, and students from rural areas. Measures relating to sensitive academic and demographic data generally require coordination with a campus office that oversees student information; it's always important to ensure that these data are handled and reported in a way that never raises even the possibility of unique student users being identified, or that may cast groups of students in an unflattering light.

Utilization data are, finally, an invaluable source of information for strategic decision making. At the broadest levels, information on who is and is not using the center can provide valuable information to guide center outreach to students and faculty, address emerging trends with programming that is responsive to students' needs, and inform decisions on resource allocation. At a more granular scale, information on when students use services can be used to set center hours, inform tutor schedules, and determine the best times for workshops and other programming. Information on who uses the center, at what times, for what duration, and for what reasons is indispensable in implementing programming that is fully responsive to learners' needs.

STUDENT SUCCESS AND LEARNING CENTER ASSESSMENT

Compiling and analyzing utilization data is a critical first step in learning center assessment, but it's not sufficient in and of itself, because the learning center's goal isn't simply to meet with students but, rather, to have a meaningful positive impact on their academic success. If learning centers and peer tutoring have value as education approaches, then we should be able to see this value when we look at the effect that our services have on the students we serve. Utilization data capture output: all of the activities that take place under the center's auspices and all of the ways in which tutors within it interact with learners. To measure impact, we must turn toward a means of assessing outcomes: the effect that these activities and interactions have on students.

OUTPUTS, OUTCOMES, AND LEARNING OUTCOMES

Learning Center Assessment and reporting may take place at any of three levels and ideally incorporates all three:

Outputs are a catalog of the activities of the center. Typical measures of output include students served, tutors employed, total interactions with learners, and the various services that the center provides. Although information on output can't directly speak to impact on students, it's valuable in providing an overview of center activities, showing changes in patterns of usage over time and the scope of the center. Combined with information on outcomes and learning outcomes, output data is important in understanding the scale of the effect that a center has on the campus it serves (e.g., Ticknor, Shaw, & Howard [2014] describe a data collection for tracking frequency of visits and demographic data of users that inform an analysis of the impact of tutoring on student grades).

Outcomes are goals that the center has articulated for itself, often informed by institutional priorities. Typical learning center outcomes are to increase student GPA, persistence, third-semester retention, and/or graduation rates for all students or for targeted groups of students. Critically, outcomes are specific and measurable, reflecting goals that the center can reasonably achieve and that can be assessed in a way that makes it possible to understand whether (or to what extent) the center is accomplishing them (e.g., Price et al., 2012; Rheinheimer & McKenzie, 2011).

Learning outcomes identify specific knowledge and skills that learners are expected to have attained by virtue of having received an educational intervention. In the context of a learning center, learning outcomes can be considered in either of two ways. Because learning centers support and reinforce classroom instruction, learning outcomes can reflect curricular outcomes (e.g., "students will be able to carry out simple experiments using the scientific method") or outcomes that correspond to academic/metacognitive skills (e.g., "students will be able to take lecture notes in which they organize and synthesize information as it is being presented"). In either case, learning outcomes, like outcomes more broadly, should be specific and measurable so that they can be assessed meaningfully (e.g., Fullmer, 2012; Hendriksen et al., 2005; Suskie, 2018).

Direct assessment of the impact that learning centers have on student success requires placing usage data in conversation with institutional information on students' success, seeking to uncover relationships between the two. Doing so requires access to institutional data on students' grades and academic performance, which, like student demographic information, is sensitive data generally overseen by a campus office that attends to institutional data and reporting. Cultivating a relationship with administrators or other professionals who can facilitate access to institutional data is a highly valuable investment in time. On many campuses the appropriate contact will be an office of assessment or of institutional analytics, staffed by individuals who can not only provide access to institutional data, but advise on strategies for assessment, consult on analytical tools, and in many cases, even run analyses (and perhaps generate reports) on the relationship between center data and institutional data.

HELPFUL RESEARCH QUESTIONS IN ANALYZING STUDENT SUCCESS DATA

Research questions focus analyses, allowing them to bring clarity to specific, predetermined issues. Research questions used for learning center assessment should be driven by each individual center's mission and goals. They may be closely related to assessment outcomes in that they pose the question of whether a particular outcome is being met.

The questions below are commonly used by learning centers and other student success programs in assessing the impact of their services on students. For all of these questions, it may be helpful to consider both center utilization as a binary variable (students who do use the center versus students who do not), and as a continuous variable (how many times students use the center). Each question could apply either to students in general, or to specific groups of students (e.g., student athletes, international students, Hispanic students, engineering majors) that are a priority for the center. In every case, they ask: What effect does learning-center usage have on students':

- grades in a particular course?
- likelihood of passing a particular course?
- success in subsequent courses (either overall, or within a specific curriculum)?
- overall GPA?
- likelihood to remain within their intended major?
- likelihood to graduate within 4 years? Within 6 years?
- likelihood to persist from their first year in college to their second?

Essentially, two levels of analysis are useful in seeking relationships between utilization data and student success data. The first, and most common, is to analyze patterns in relationships between students' use of peer tutoring and academic outcomes. Comparisons between groups of students (e.g., looking at the overall GPAs of students who do and do not make use of the center in a given academic year), or correlations between center use and academic success (e.g., the correlation, between the time students in a particular course spend in the learning center and their final course grade). The second is to use statistical analyses (such as t-tests, ANOVAs, and significance testing of correlational coefficients) to determine whether differences between groups, or correlations between variables, rise to the level of statistical significance rather than being attributable to random variation that occurs in all data sets. The results of analyses such as these provide a valuable indication of whether a center is having the desired impact on the students who use it, and patterns that align with expectations can offer valuable support for the hypothesis that use of the services within the center leads to greater academic success for students. They can also speak, as it applies to the center's student staff, to the academic benefits of peer tutoring for tutors themselves. Bolstered by other sources of assessment data, such as survey data, they can make a powerful case for the benefit of the center for learners and the impact that the center has on campus.

THE PROBLEM OF SELF-SELECTION
BIAS IN LEARNING CENTER ASSESSMENT

The classic problem in assessment of learning centers and other student success programs is causality: because the students who use peer tutoring self-select to do so, how do we know that an observed relationship between students' use of the center and increased academic success (higher GPA, faster graduation, etc.) is due to support they received as opposed to students' inherent attributes? To put it another way: How can we know that students who use the center's services weren't bound to succeed anyway simply because they are the type of student who has the self-efficacy to use peer tutoring?

Researchers have applied a number of innovative approaches to addressing this issue. Bowles, McCoy, and Bates (2008) used a system-of-equations statistical model incorporating both SAT scores and high school GPA to account for the effect of self-selection bias, finding that freshmen SI attendance increases the probability of timely graduation by 11% even when other factors are taken into account. Gattis (2003) used a method that controlled both for predictors of academic success (entrance exam scores, high school GPA), and used a motivation-matched control group (comprising students who wanted to attend SI sessions but were unable to due to schedule conflicts) to remove other factors from the analysis, finding that attendance at SI session had an effect of about a quarter of a letter grade even beyond attendees' inherent motivation and academic preparedness. Colver and Fry (2016) used a nonequivalent comparison group design to approximate an experimental setup in which students of similar levels of motivation either were or were not provided with peer tutoring. Drawing on a large set of institutional data, they compared students who 1) had taken a course and received a low grade, repeated it, and used peer tutoring on the second attempt; and 2) had taken a course and received a low grade, repeated it, and not used peer tutoring on the second attempt. Their finding was that peer tutoring had a significant effect on the course grade of students who did use tutoring in their second attempt of a course.

Numerous other statistical methods can be used for isolating the effect of peer tutoring from other confounding variables related to background, abilities, and inherent traits that affect students' success. They include post-hoc t-tests that compare groups of students who used the center to groups of students with similar predictors of academic success (high school grades, entrance exam scores, etc.) and multiple regressions that analyze the individual effect of multiple causal factors (including, for example, students' use not only of peer tutoring but also other support services). Very likely individuals in your campus's office of assessment and/or institutional analytics are available to offer support in the endeavor of doing so. You don't necessarily need statistical savvy to be great at assessment as long as you have the savvy to make connections on campus to those who do!

SURVEY DATA

Data gleaned from surveys of students can provide important qualitative data, filling in gaps in assessment that can be left unfilled by the more quantitative sources. Survey data is, by nature, subjective. Although analyses that correlate utilization data with students' success data provide a more objective and direct measure of the effect of center activities on learners, survey data addresses this relationship only indirectly, evaluating learners' *perceptions* of the impact of the support they receive rather than the impact itself. Nonetheless, in the answers that students and other stakeholders provide in response to questions about the center, they reveal information that can be vital to understanding the patterns observed in utilization and success data and can provide a much more well-rounded picture of the center than would be attainable through quantitative data alone.

Gauging the satisfaction of student users is one important goal of learning center surveys. Questions that assess recent attendees' feelings about their sessions in the center (e.g., "On a scale of 1 to 5, how satisfied are you with your visit to the center?"; "Did you find your tutor helpful? Why or why not?") are among the most common types of questions in center surveys. Students' answers to satisfaction questions give feedback on center services, specific programs, and individual tutors, providing deeply important insight into how students experience their visits to the center (often pointing toward specific, implementable feedback that can be used to improve the way that students experience the center). It can also be used (if students identify the tutor[s] who they worked with) as a source of feedback on individual tutors, and many centers use survey data either as an important data point for tutor evaluations or simply as a source of kudos to be passed along to tutors to show how much learners appreciate their work.

On the other hand, it's important to remember that satisfaction survey data should always be taken with a grain of salt. Peer tutors are always, in their work with learners, walking a fine line between meeting students' needs and making sure that learners are doing the majority of the work (and therefore learning) in a session. And it's important to consider what student satisfaction means in the context of the learning center: it would be possible for a tutoring interaction to leave a student user highly satisfied with a center visit precisely because it does not follow the pedagogical framework of peer tutoring (e.g., because a writing tutor edited a student's paper), or for a user to be dissatisfied precisely because a tutor successfully implemented the strategies they were trained to use (e.g., redirecting a question to a student user rather than providing an answer). Student satisfaction is one important measure of a center, but it can't by itself provide a complete picture, and it should be carefully considered if and how satisfaction data bears on the question of whether a center is fulfilling its mission and goals.

Surveys play a deeper role when they are used to assess outcomes. Survey data on students' perceptions of the ways that visits to the center affect them (e.g., students' impressions of how peer tutoring impacted their study habits, writing ability, problem-solving skills, or confidence in their ability to succeed) can, especially in combination with quantitative data, indicate in fine-grained detail the extent of and ways in which the programming within the center contributes to academic success. Questions on students' attitudes following tutoring sessions can indicate ways in which students' visits to the center affect their feelings of inclusion, involvement, and engagement, important factors in students' persistence in college. For reporting purposes, student testimonials ("I couldn't have passed molecular biology without the learning center! The tutors helped me to understand the dense terminology in the textbook and to figure out how to solve problems for myself") and survey data in which student users speak to the effect that peer tutoring has had on their studies (e.g., "94% of student users felt that their visit to the center made them more likely to meet their academic goals") are among the most powerful ways to supplement student success data in a way that speaks to a causal relationship between center usage and positive outcomes.

Surveys can be distributed in a number of ways. One relatively simple and common method is to have feedback forms available to students, either on paper or on a dedicated device, near the point where students exit the center (one variation, available through some tutor scheduling platforms, is to have a survey option that appears for students as they log out of the center). Another is to e-mail a survey link to students who have made recent use of the center (the ability to do so automatically is, again, an option through some tutor scheduling platforms).

A major issue with these relatively passive approaches is that they tend to produce a pattern of bimodal distribution in the survey responses: in the absence of any particular incentive to complete a survey, student users tend to do so only when they are either extremely happy or extremely unhappy with the service that they received. Students in the middle, likely representing the majority of users, end up underrepresented in the results. One solution is to incentivize participation, offering an external motivation for participation (e.g., entry in a raffle to win $50 credit at the college bookstore). Another, perhaps complementary approach is to focus surveying on certain busy times during the semester (e.g., a "survey week" that occurs around the time of midterm exams) during which survey participation is heavily advertised and sincerely invited— ideally, and most effectively, by tutors themselves. Any approach that creates greater participation is to the good, as a larger sample—provided participation

SAMPLE POST-VISIT SURVEY FOR STUDENT USERS

Thank you for visiting the learning center! Please take a few moments to let us know about your visit; we use this information to help recognize the efforts of the tutors and improve our services. This survey takes about 3–5 minutes to complete. Thank you in advance for your time.

1. Which service did you use today?
   - ☐ Individual appointment
   - ☐ Drop-in lab
   - ☐ SI session

2. How satisfied were you with your visit to the center?

   Not at all satisfied   1   2   3   4   5   Extremely satisfied

   Is there anything more you'd like to tell us about your response?

3. In your visit, did you receive the help that you were hoping to receive?
   - ☐ Yes
   - ☐ No

   Is there anything more you'd like to tell us about your response?

4. Did the tutor(s) who you worked with ask questions that gave you the chance to explain your understanding of the material you were seeking support for?

   Not at all   1   2   3   4   5   Very much

5. As a result of your visit to the center, do you feel more confident in your ability to succeed in the course for which you were seeking support?

   Not at all   1   2   3   4   5   Very much

6. As a result of your visit to the center, do you feel more confident in your ability to succeed in your planned course of study?

   Not at all   1   2   3   4   5   Very much

7. For each topic below, please indicate the extent to which your visit to the center helped you build new strategies that you expect to apply in your future coursework:

	Not at all			Very much
Strategies for taking notes	1	2	3	4	5
Strategies for studying	1	2	3	4	5
Strategies for managing my time	1	2	3	4	5
Strategies for solving problems	1	2	3	4	5

8. Is there anything else you'd like to tell us about your visit to the center?

9. Do you have any specific suggestions on how we can improve our services?

is not incentivized in a way likely to bias the results—always provides a more powerful representative sample of a population than a smaller one.

One other concern in garnering participation is survey length. Although longer surveys can obviously garner far more complete and thorough data than shorter ones, an exhaustive approach comes at a heavy cost in terms of participation: the longer a survey, the fewer students will complete it. A survey that students can dash off in a minute or two will generally have a much higher response rate than one that takes longer to complete. Similarly, questions that students can answer with a rating (e.g., a Likert scale in which students rate their satisfaction with their tutoring experience on a scale from 1 to 5) will generally get a higher response rate than questions soliciting a prose response. Such questions also have the benefit of responses that can be easily compiled and averaged across a large number of participants. On the other hand, students' prose responses often offer valuable, specific information that can't be captured with a simple rating. For this reason, surveys often take the approach of first inviting a rating (e.g., "To what extent do you feel that your visit to the center increased your confidence that you will pass the course you sought support for?") and then provide participants with the option to add further explanation with a prose response. ("If you would care to, please explain your response here.")

Importantly, center users are not the only potential target of surveys. In many cases, and in particular when assessment data is being used to strategize outreach efforts, it can be more valuable to learn about impressions of the center among students who do *not* use it: what keeps them from doing so? Do they know about the center and its services? What misapprehensions about the center might they hold? What attitudes do they have about peer tutoring or academic support more broadly? Surveys of other groups of stakeholders— faculty, academic advisors, student affairs professionals, and staff in other student-serving programs—on their impressions of the center, the scenarios in which they might refer a student for services, and their attitudes toward the center can all play an important role in assessing the center's marketing and outreach efforts and in gaining insight into how our programs are perceived on the campuses we serve. Finally, surveys of tutors can yield invaluable information on the benefits of peer tutoring for the students who serve as peer educators, as well as data that can be used for the purposes of assessing the center's employment practices and tutor training program/curriculum.

A SUGGESTED PROCESS FOR AN ANNUAL ASSESSMENT CYCLE

The point of assessment is not, ultimately, to gather data, but rather to inform decision making. It's critical, in order to make effective use of assessment data, to set aside time for drawing meaning from it and to devote as much time and intentionality to using assessment data as is devoted to collecting it. A well-planned assessment cycle places operational improvements, strategic planning, and assessment data in relation to one another, allowing an LCA to make data-informed decisions, plan effectively, and use information gleaned from assessment as feedback on the effectiveness of programmatic changes in achieving center outcomes. The plan below outlines an annual assessment cycle; it could just as easily take place on a term-by-term basis. Critically, assessment is iterative, with assessment resulting in program changes that are, in turn, assessed. The fundamentals of the center should be assessed repeatedly over time to ensure that the center is attaining its core goals.

Before the Academic Year Begins, Create a List of Desired Outcomes

A list of desired outcomes is the key to designing your assessment measures and interpreting your results. It should encompass goals (e.g., increase student usage), strategic planning (e.g., improve the tutor training program so that tutors use more active learning approaches with learners), and outcomes (e.g., increase awareness of metacognitive strategies among students in the social sciences).

At the Beginning of the Academic Year, Create an Assessment Plan

Use your list of desired outcomes to create a list of research questions. Throughout the year, how will you gather usage, student success, and survey data in a way to allow you to determine the center's effectiveness in meeting its goals? What other measures of usage will be useful for reporting and strategic planning?

Throughout the Academic Year, Implement the Assessment Plan

Deploy instruments on a predetermined schedule, gather information on a regular basis, and monitor assessment data on a continuous basis. Throughout the year, gather and archive assessment data as it is received. It's not yet time for a deep dive into assessment data, but be sure to set aside time (e.g., a monthly staff meeting, or a dedicated day after each major survey cycle) to review utilization and survey data, which can be important sources of information for responding to emerging issues that may require an immediate response (e.g., spikes in usage at certain times of day when more tutors are needed, growing dissatisfaction among student users from a certain discipline).

At the End of the Academic Year, Analyze Data and Set Goals for the Upcoming Cycle

Work through the goals articulated at the beginning of the year, determining how the assessment data gathered throughout the year speaks to the center's success in attaining them (and consider necessary changes).

At this stage, you're taking a deep dive into all of the data you've collected. Gather all of the needed student success data to complete necessary analyses and consider how your data speaks to your research questions. Based on the data you've collected, where is the center attaining its goals? Where is it falling short? Look at your data critically: how could the center more effectively attain its goals in the year ahead? Articulate these as planned programmatic changes for the following cycle. You're also ready to complete all necessary reporting.

ASSESSMENT REPORTING

In assessment reports, we draw on assessment data to create a summary account of the activities of the center. Critically, learning center reports are not repositories of data but arguments that draw on assessment data to persuade an audience. Effective assessment practices and regularly tracking utilization can result in incredible amounts of information. A well-crafted assessment report doesn't require a reader to wade through all of this data—it summarizes general patterns and isolates key pieces of information, presenting them in a way that gives the reader a brief, accurate summary of the center's activities, its impact on campus, and the way it addresses concerns that the reader cares about.

In gathering assessment data, input comes from a variety of categories (the major ones being utilization data, analyses based on student success data, and survey data). In reporting assessment data, these categories do not matter so much as does the narrative that is created for the audience. An effective assessment report doesn't move in chronological or categorical progression through sources of data, but, rather, it presents a narrative that organizes information in a way that supports the argument being made. Assessment reports should be organized according to outcomes, demonstrating how centers are attaining the goals they or the institution set (or, alternately, how they are falling short of doing so and will seek to do so in the future).

Because reports are crafted for audiences, reports written for different audiences may take very different forms. College and university administrators are concerned with advancing institutional outcomes. Accordingly, required annual reports created for administrative overseers should be organized around the ways that the center advances the strategic priorities of the administrative unit to which the center reports. Reports written for other groups of stakeholders (e.g., customized reports for individual academic units, a summary "report card" on the center sent to all faculty, reports for student government) can and should take very different forms according to the interests and goals of the intended audience. Every assessment report should proceed not from the prompt "What information do I have?" but from the question "What does my audience care about?," establishing basic information on size, impact, and growth before moving on briskly to outcomes.

SAMPLE ANNUAL REPORT

The Learning Center at Hypothetical University is a full-service learning center offering peer tutoring for students across the academic disciplines. Through individual appointments, drop-in labs, workshops, online tutoring, and an SI program, the Learning Center supports students as learners, writers, and problem solvers.

The Learning Center is a well-regarded program with far-reaching impact at Hypothetical University. In AY 2020/2021:

- 2,246 HU students (28% of the student body) visited the Learning Center at least once.
- The 67 students who serve as peer educators engaged in more than ten thousand contact hours with HU students.
- 89% of students who visited the Learning Center indicated a high degree of satisfaction with their experience, and 92% of students who visited the Learning Center indicated that they would recommend the service to another student.

Based on our mission and current strategic priorities, our assessment efforts for AY 2020/2021 academic were focused on three outcomes:

Outcome 1: Increase Academic Success for All Students

- Students who used the Learning Center at least once averaged an overall GPA .42 higher than their peers who did not use the center, and there was a significant correlation (.47) between students' total number of visits to the center and their overall GPA.
- In a multiple regression analysis that looked at the number of times students visited the center, SAT/ACT score, and high school GPA as factors in students' overall college success, peer tutoring was a significant ($p < .05$) predictor of overall GPA.
- On a scale of 1 to 5, a representative sample of student users ($n = 237$) averaged a response of 4.62 to the question "As a result of your visit to the

center, do you feel more confident in your ability to succeed in the course for which you received support?"

Outcome 2: Increase Academic Skills for Students in All Disciplines

- 97% of student user survey respondents indicated improvement in at least one of the following areas as a result of their visit to the center: note taking, time management, problem solving, approaching large projects, studying.
- In a survey of HU faculty, 72% of respondents indicated that students who were referred to the center subsequently demonstrated stronger application of academic skills such as note taking and time management.

Outcome 3: Support Institutional Efforts to Retain URM Natural Science Majors

- URM students who used the Learning Center at least once in Chemistry 101, Biology 101, or Physics 101 were 19% less likely to withdraw from or fail the course.
- URM students who used the Learning Center at least once in Chemistry 101, Sociology 101, or Physics 101 were 37% more likely to receive a grade of B or better in the second course in the sequence (Chemistry 102, Sociology 102, or Physics 102, respectively).
- In a survey of upper-division URM students in natural science majors ($n = 172$), 32% of respondents identified the Learning Center as a factor in their ability to succeed in their major. Asked to explain their responses further, a number of students described the value of working with tutors from their own minority group who could serve as mentors and guides to the discipline.

Effective assessment practices empower us to administer our centers with a clear-eyed, objective, and complex understanding of the programs we lead. The literature of academic success and learning center theory offers a robust set of best practices that have been repeatedly demonstrated to have a significant, positive impact on learners. Assessment offers the tools to ensure that these best practices are being implemented in a way that will maximize their full benefit, as well as to communicate these benefits in a way that will resonate with external stakeholders of the center.

QUESTIONS FOR PROGRAM ASSESSMENT

General

- Do the center's assessment methods provide a basis for determining whether (and to what extent) the center is fulfilling its mission?

- Do the center's assessment methods provide a basis for making strategic decision making on issues such as hiring, scheduling, space use, and long-term planning?
- Do the center's assessment methods make use of a combination of utilization, student success, and survey data, providing multiple measures and perspectives on the impact of the center?
- Are the center's assessment methods organized around clearly articulated outcomes?
- Does the center have an assessment cycle that dedicates time to planning, implementing, and making changes in response to assessment?

Utlization Data

- Is student utilization recorded in a way that provides accurate, fine-grained information on every visit (including duration and purpose), and on every student (including an identifier that can be link each student's identity to campus repositories of student data)?
- Do the center's assessment methods allow for breakdowns and analyses of student users based on demographic information (gender, race, etc.)?
- Are the center's methods for tracking usage consistent from term to term, so that they can be used to measure change over time?
- Is utilization data collected and analyzed in a way that is informed by assessment outcomes, and allows the center to determine whether (and to what extent) it is meeting them?

Student Success Data

- Are the center's assessment methods driven by research questions that focus on specific issues that can be meaningfully addressed and are connected to center and institutional priorities?
- Do the center's assessment methods use multiple forms of valid analyses to determine the relationship between center services and student success, mitigating as much as possible the role of other factors in student success?
- Are analyses of student success data completed in a way that is informed by assessment outcomes and allows the center to determine whether (and to what extent) it is meeting them?

Surveys

- Do survey data provide a measure of student satisfaction with center services?

- Do survey data provide a measure of the effect of tutoring on students' learning, attitudes, academic skills, or other desired outcomes?
- Are surveys implemented in a way that provides a sufficiently large sample of student users that represents a wide cross-section of student users?

Reporting

- Do the center's reports briefly provide enough usage data to understand the scale and scope of the center?
- Is the center's reporting organized around outcomes, presenting assessment data in a way that addresses the center's goals?
- Does the center's reporting address the goals and priorities of the audience(s) for which it is written?

Epilogue

Learning center administration is work that makes a difference. In doing our work with creativity, passion, and attentiveness to the lessons of experience and openness to new directions, we have the greatest possible positive impact on campuses we serve—and, collectively, on higher education as a whole. We've attempted in these chapters to provide a set of principles, based on our own experiences and on the body of knowledge that has been developed in the scholarship of peer-led learning, to support you in this. What's missing, and what only you can supply, is the particular insight you offer based on your experiences as to how they can best be applied (as well as where they must be developed, challenged, or problematized) at your institution.

There is a lot here! In using this book as a guide for program assessment, and in informing programmatic goals, determine where your center's needs are most urgent, consider where your efforts will be most impactful, decide in what order priorities should be tackled, allocate a realistic amount of time for accomplishing outcomes, and develop a multiyear plan. Moving a program toward excellence isn't the work of a year; it's the work of a career. Every step is important, and every term in which the center is moved meaningfully closer to the goal of overall excellence is a good one. In approaching this work as a scholar-administrator, draw on the enormous body of relevant knowledge—a selected portion of which we have distilled here—to inform the choices that you make. And return to it in kind, contributing through conference presentations and publication to the collected knowledge of our field, driving our successors to make yet more empowered choices. Through our combined efforts, we as a community can foster a culture of learning not only on our own campuses but on *every* campus, transforming higher education as a whole to become as broadly inclusive, individually attentive, and collectively empowering as possible.

References

ACT. (2010). What works in student retention? Public four-year colleges and universities report. http://www.act.org/research/policymakers/pdf/droptables/PublicFour -YrColleges.pdf

Americans with Disabilities Act. (1990). Pub. L. No. 101-336, 104 Stat. 328.

Anderson, E., & Kim, D. (2006). Increasing the success of minority students in science and technology. Washington, DC: American Council on Education.

Arco-Tirado, J., Fernández-Martín, F., & Fernández-Balboa, J. (2011). The impact of a peer-tutoring program on quality standards in higher education. *Higher Education, 62*(6), 773–788.

Arendale, D. (2004). Mainstreamed academic assistance and enrichment for all students: The historical origins of learning assistance centers. *Research for Educational Reform, 9*(4), 3–21.

The Association of College and Research Libraries. (2000). Information Literacy Competency Standards for Higher Education. Retrieved from https://alair .ala.org/bitstream/handle/11213/7668/ACRL%20Information%20Literacy%20 Competency%20Standards%20for%20Higher%20Education.pdf?sequence=1 &isAllowed=y

Bailey, G. K. (2010). *Tutoring strategies: A case study comparing learning center tutors and academic department tutors* (Doctoral dissertation). Available from ProQuest Dissertations and Theses database (UMI No. 3403672). Retrieved from http://www.lsche.net/assets/Bailey_Geoffrey_dissertation_4-7-10.pdf

Bannier, B. (2007). Predicting mathematics learning center visits: An examination of correlating variables. *Learning Assistance Review, 12*(1), 7–16.

Beagle, D. (with contributions by D. R. Bailey & B. Tierney). (2006). *Information commons handbook*. New York, NY: Neal-Schuman.

Beasley, C. (1997). Students as teachers: The benefits of peer tutoring. *Teaching and Learning Forum, 97*, 21–30.

Bell, B., & Stutts, R. (1997). The road to hell is paved with good intentions: The effects of mandatory writing center visits on student and tutor attitudes. *Writing Lab Newsletter, 22*(1), 5–8.

Benjamin, A. S., & Tullis, J. (2010). What makes distributed practice effective? *Cognitive Psychology, 61*, 228–247.

Bennett, S. (2003). *Libraries designed for learning.* Washington, DC: Council on Library and Information Resources. http://www.clir.org/pubs/abstract/pub122abst.html

Berghmans, I., Neckebroeck, F., Dochy, F., & Struyven, K. (2013). A typology of approaches to peer tutoring. Unraveling peer tutors' behavioural strategies. *European Journal of Psychology of Education, 28*, 703–723.

Bishop, W. (1990). Bringing writers to the center: Some survey results, surmises, and suggestions. *Writing Center Journal, 10*(2), 31–44.

Blanc, R. A., DeBuhr, L., & Martin, D. C. (1983). Breaking the attrition cycle: The effects of Supplemental Instruction on undergraduate performance and attrition. *Journal of Higher Education, 54*(1), 80–89.

Bleakney, J. (2019). Ongoing writing tutor education: Models and practices. In K. G. Johnson & T. Roggenbuck, *How we teach writing tutors: A WLN digital edited collection.* https://wlnjournal.org/digitaleditedcollection1/Bleakney.html

Bonwell, C. C., & Eison, J. A. (1991). Active learning: Creating excitement in the classroom. ASH#-ERIC Higher Education Report No. 1. Washington, DC: George Washington University, School of Education and Human Development.

Boquet, E. (1999). "Our little secret": A history of writing centers, pre- to post-open admissions. *College Composition and Communication, 50*(3), 463–482. doi: 10.2307/358861

Boquet, E. (2001). *Noise from the writing center.* Logan, UT: Utah State Press.

Bourelle, A. (2007). The first-year composition requirement: An important introduction to the writing center. *Praxis: A Writing Center Journal 4*(2). https://reposito ries.lib.utexas.edu/bitstream/handle/2152/62405/Bourelle_%204.2WritingCenter AndTheClassroom-7.pdf?sequence=2&isAllowed=y

Bowles, T. J., McCoy A. C., & Bates, S. C. (2008). The effect of supplemental instruction on timely graduation. *College Student Journal, 42*(30), 853–859.

Boylan, H. R., Bliss, L. B., & Bonham, B. S. (1997). Program components and their relationship to student performance. *Journal of Developmental Education, 20*(3), 2–6.

Boylan, H. R., Bonham, B. S., Bliss, L. B., & Saxon, D. P. (1995). What we know about tutoring: Findings from the national study of developmental education. *Research in Developmental Education, 21*(3), 1–4.

Breslin, J. D., Hope, M. K., O'Hatnick, J. L., & Sharpe, A. G. (2018). Students as colleagues: A paradigm for understanding student leaders in academic support. *Learning Assistance Review, 23*(2), 41–64.

Brooks, Jeff. (1991). Minimalist tutoring: Making the student do all the work. *Writing Lab Newsletter, 15*(6), 1–4.

Brown, M., & Long, P. (2006). Trends in learning space design. In D. Oblinger (Ed.), *Learning spaces.* Washington, DC: EDUCAUSE.

Bruffee, K. (1984). Collaborative learning and the "conversation of mankind." *College English, 46*(7), 635–652. doi:10.2307/376924

Bunting, B. D. (2014). *Being transformed by being a peer mentor: An examination of high-impact and transformative peer mentor experience* (Unpublished doctoral dissertation). Brigham Young University, Provo, UT.

Burgstahler, S. (2017). *Equal access: Universal design of tutoring and learning centers.* https://www.washington.edu/doit/sites/default/files/atoms/files/EA_Tu toring_Learning_Centers.pdf

Burmeister, S. L., Kenney, P. A., & Nice, D. L. (1996). Analysis of effectiveness of Supplemental Instruction sessions for college algebra, calculus, and statistics. In J. J. Kaput, A. H. Schoenfeld, & E. Dubinsky (Eds.), *Research in collegiate mathematics education II* (pp. 145–154). Providence, RI: American Mathematical Association and Mathematical Association of America.

Burnett, D., & Oblinger, D. (2003). Student academic services: Models, current practices, and trends. In G. L. Kramer (Ed.), *Student academic services: An integrated approach* (pp. 27–52). San Francisco, CA: Jossey-Bass.

Cai, Q., Lewis, C. L., & Higdon, J. (2015). Developing an early-alert system to promote student visits to tutor center. *Learning Assistance Review, 20*(1), 61–72.

Capar, G., & Tarim, K. (2015). Efficacy of the cooperative learning method on mathematics achievement and attitude: A meta-analysis research. *Educational Sciences: Theory and Practice, 15*(2), 553–559.

Carpenter, S. K., & Mueller, F. E. (2013). The effects of interleaving versus blocking on foreign language pronunciation learning. *Memory & Cognition, 41*, 671–682. doi:10.3758/s13421-012-0291-4

Cepeda, N. J., Pashler, H., Vul, E., Wixted, J. T., & Rohrer, D. (2006). Distributed practice in verbal recall tasks: A review and quantitative synthesis. *Psychological Bulletin, 132*(3), 354–380.

Chadwick, S. A., & McGuire, S. P. (2004). Effect of relational communication training for tutors on tutee course grades. *Learning Assistance Review, 9*(2), 29–40.

Cheatle, J., & Bullerjahn, M. (2015). Undergraduate student perceptions and the writing center. *WLN: A Journal of Writing Center Scholarship, 40*(1–2), 19–26.

Chester, A., Burton, L. J., Xenos, S. & Elgar, K. (2013). Peer mentoring: Supporting successful transition for first year undergraduate psychology students. *Australian Journal of Psychology, 65*, 30–37.

Chick, N. L., Haynie, A., & Gurung, R. A. R. (2009). From generic to signature pedagogies. In R. A. R. Gurung, N. L. Chick, & A. Haynie (Eds.), *Exploring signature pedagogies: Approaches to teaching disciplinary habits of mind.* Sterling, VA: Stylus.

Chickering, A. W., & Gamson, Z. F. (1987). Seven principles for good practice in undergraduate education. *AAHE Bulletin,* March, 3–7.

Chilvers, L. (2016). Communities of practice for international students: An exploration of the role of peer assisted study sessions in supporting transition and learning in higher education. *Journal of Learning Development in Higher Education, 10*, 1–25.

Chisholm W., Vanderheiden G., & Jacobs, I. (2001). Web content accessibility guidelines. *Interactions, 8*(4).

Christ, F. L. (1971). Systems for learning assistance: Learners, learning facilitators, and learning centers. In F. L. Christ (Ed.), *Interdisciplinary aspects of reading instruction, proceedings of the fourth annual conference of the Western College Reading Association, 4*, 32–41.

Clark, I. (1985). Leading the horse: The writing center and required visits. *Writing Center Journal, 5*(2), 31–34.

Clark, I. (1988). Collaboration and ethics in writing center pedagogy. *Writing Center Journal, 9*(1), 3–12.

Coe, E. M., McDougall, A. O., & McKeown, N. B. (1999). Is peer assisted learning of benefit to undergraduate chemists? *University Chemistry Education, 3*(2), 72–75.

Cohen, P. A., & Kulik, J. A. (1981). Synthesis of research on the effects of tutoring. *Educational Leadership, 39*(3), 227–229.

Colver, M., & Fry, T. (2016). Evidence to support peer tutoring programs at the undergraduate level. *Journal of College Reading and Learning, 46*(1), 16–41. doi:10 .1080/10790195.2015.1075446.

Colvin, J. (2007). Peer tutoring and social dynamics in higher education. *Mentoring and Tutoring, 15*(2), 165–181.

Comfort, P., & McMahon, J. J. (2014). The effect of peer tutoring on academic achievement. *Journal of Applied Research in Higher Education, 6*(1), 168–175. doi:10.1108/JARHE-06-2012-0017

Cooper, E. (2010). Tutoring center effectiveness: The effect of drop-in tutoring. *Journal of College Reading and Learning, 40*(2), 21–34. doi:10.1080/10790195 .2010.10850328

Cooperative Institutional Research Program at the Higher Education Research Institute at UCLA. (2018). The American freshman: National norms. Retrieved from https://www.heri.ucla.edu/monographs/TheAmericanFreshman2018.pdf

Craig, A., Richardson, E., & Harris, J. (2018). Learning center advisory boards: Results of an online exploratory survey. *Learning Assistance Review, 23*(2), 87–114.

Cromley, J. G., & Azevedo, R. (2005). What do reading tutors do? A naturalistic study of more and less experienced tutors in reading [electronic version]. *Discourse Processes, 40*(2), 83–113.

Crouch, C. H., & Mazur, E. (2001). Peer instruction: Ten years of experience and results. *American Journal of Physics, 69*, 970–977.

Dawson, K. (2009). Principles of academic success and mentorship: An interview with Saundra McGuire. *Journal of Developmental Education, 33*(2), 22–25.

Deacon, S. H., Tucker, R., Bergey, B. W., Laroche, A., & Parrila, R. (2017). Personalized outreach to university students with a history of reading difficulties: Early screening and outreach to support academically at-risk students. *Journal of College Student Development, 58*(3), 432–450. doi:10.1353/csd.2017.0032

DeFeo, D. J., Bonin, D., & Ossiander-Gobeille, M. (2017). Waiting and help-seeking in math tutoring exchanges. *Journal of Developmental Education, 40*(3), 14–22.

Denny, H. (2010). Queering the writing center. *Writing Center Journal, 30*(1), 95–124.

Devet, B. (2006). The good, the bad, and the ugly of certifying a tutoring program through CRLA. In C. Murphy and B. Stay (Eds.), *The writing center director's resource book* (pp. 331–337). Mahwah, NJ: Laurence Erlbaum.

Devirian, M. C., Enright, G., & Smith, G. D. (1975). A survey of learning program centers in U.S. institutions of higher education. In R. Sugimoto (Ed.), *College learning skills today and tomorrowland.* Proceedings of the eighth annual conference of the Western College Reading Association (vol. 8, 69–76).

Durkin, K., & Main, A. (2002). Discipline-based study skills support for first-year undergraduate students. *Active Learning in Higher Education, 3*(1), 24–39.

Earl, W. R. (1988). Intrusive advising of freshmen in academic difficulty [electronic version]. *NACADA Journal, 8*(2), 27–33.

Ede, L. (1989). Writing as social process: A theoretical foundation for writing centers? *Writing Center Journal, 9*(2), 3–13.

Edwards, D. F., & Thatcher, J. (2004). A student-centred tutor-led approach to teaching research methods. *Journal of Further and Higher Education, 28*(2), 195–206. doi:10.1080/0309877042000206750

Eimers, M. (2000). Assessing the impact of the early alert program. AIR 2000 Annual Forum Paper. (ERIC Document Reproduction Service No. ED446511). https://eric .ed.gov/?id=ED446511

Etter, E. R., Burmeister, S. L., & Elder, R. J. (2000). Improving student performance and retention via supplemental instruction. *Journal of Accounting Education, 18,* 355–368.

Fagen, A. P., Crouch, C. H., & Mazur, E. (2002). Peer instruction: Results from a range of classrooms. *Physics Teacher, 40,* 206–209.

Fantuzzo, J. W., Dimeff, L. A., & Fox, S. L. (1989). Reciprocal peer tutoring: A multimodal assessment of effectiveness with college students. *Teaching of Psychology, 16*(3), 133–135.

Fantuzzo, J. W., Riggio, R. E., Connelly, S., & Dimeff, L. A. (1989). Effects of reciprocal peer tutoring on academic achievement and psychological adjustment: A component analysis. *Journal of Educational Psychology, 81*(2), 173–177.

Forester, J. P., Thomas, P. P., & McWhorter, D. L. (2004). Effects of four supplemental instruction programs on students' learning of gross anatomy. *Clinical Anatomy, 17*(4), 322–327.

Forrest, C., & Hinchliffe, J. L. (2005). Beyond classroom construction and design: Formulating a vision for learning spaces in libraries. *Reference & User Services Quarterly, 44,* 296–301.

Franks, J. A., & Tosko, M. P. (2007). Reference librarians speak for users: A learning commons concept that meets the needs of a diverse student body. *Reference Librarian, 47,* 105–118.

Freeman, S., Eddy, S. L., McDonough, M., Smith, M. K., Okoroafor, N., Jordt, H., & Wenderoth, M. P. (2014). Active learning increases student performance in science, engineering, and mathematics. *Proceedings of the National Academy of Sciences, 111*(23), 8410–8841.

Fullmer, P. (2012). Assessment of tutoring laboratories in a learning assistance center. *Journal of College Reading and Learning, 42*(2), 67–89.

Gabelnick, F., MacGregor, J., Matthews, R. S., & Smith, B. L. (1990). Learning communities: Creating connections among students, faculty, and disciplines. *New Directions for Teaching and Learning, 41.* San Francisco, CA: Jossey-Bass.

Galbraith, J., & Winterbottom, M. (2011). Peer-tutoring: What's in it for the tutor? *Educational Studies, 37*(3). doi:10.1080/03055698.2010.506330

Gardner, H. (2006). *Multiple intelligences: New horizons.* New York, NY: Basic Books.

Gattis, K. W. (2002). Responding to self-selection bias in assessments of academic support programs: A motivational control study of supplemental instruction. *Learning Assistance Review, 7*(2), 26–36.

Gentle, C., Shaw, R., & Scott, S. (2015). Reflective journals as a developmental tool in PAL. *Journal of Learning Development in Higher Education.* Special Edition: Academic Peer Learning. Accessed at https://journal.aldinhe.ac.uk/index.php/jldhe/article/view/372/pdf

Goldstein, J., Sauer, P., & O'Donnell, J. (2014). Understanding factors leading to participation in supplemental instruction programs in introductory accounting courses. *Accounting Education, 23*(6), 507–526. doi:10.1080/09639284.2014.963132

Gordon, B. (2008). Requiring first-year writing classes to visit the writing center: Bad attitudes or positive results? *Teaching English in the Two-Year College, 36*(2), 154–163.

Graesser, A. C., Person, N. K., & Magliano, J. P. (1995). Collaborative dialogue patterns in naturalistic one-to-one tutoring. *Applied Cognitive Psychology, 9,* 495–522.

Graetz, K. A. (2006). The psychology of learning environments. In D. Oblinger (Ed.), *Learning spaces.* Washington, DC: EDUCAUSE.

Green, N. (2018). Moving beyond alright: And the emotional toll of this, my life matters too, in the writing center work. *Writing Center Journal, 37*(1), 15–34.

Green, T. (2007). Organizational transformation to meet and exceed service expectations: The role of one-stop centers in higher education. Washington, DC: AACRAO Consulting.

Greene, T. G., Marti, C. N., & McClennney, K. (2008). The effort-outcome gap: Differences for African American and Hispanic community college students in student engagement and academic achievement. *Journal of Higher Education, 79*(5), 513–539.

Grillo, M. C., & Leist, C. W. (2014). Academic support as a predictor of retention to graduation: New insights on the role of tutoring, learning assistance, and supplemental instruction. *Journal of College Student Retention, 15*(3), 387–408.

Grutsch McKinney, K. (2005). Leaving home sweet home: Towards critical readings of writing center spaces. *Writing Center Journal, 25*(2), 6–20.

Haak, D. C., HilleRisLambers, J., Pitre, E., & Freeman, S. (2011). Increased structure and active learning reduce the achievement gap in introductory biology. *Science, 332,* 1213–1216.

Habley, W. R., Bloom, J. L., & Robbins, S. (2012). *Increasing persistence: Research-based strategies for college student success.* San Francisco, CA: Jossey-Bass.

Hake, R. R. (1998). Interactive-engagement versus traditional methods: A six-thousand-student survey of mechanics test data for introductory physics courses. *American Journal of Physics, 66*(1), 64.

Hartman, H. (1990). Factors affecting the tutoring process. *Journal of Developmental Education, 14*(2), 2–16.

Harris, M. (1988). SLATE (Support for the Learning and Teaching of English) statement: The concept of a writing center. Urbana, IL: National Council of Teachers of English.

Harris, M. (1986). *Teaching one-to-one: The writing conference.* Urbana, IL: National Council of Teachers of English.

Healy, D. (1995). Writing center directors: An emerging portrait of the profession. *Writing Program Administration, 18*(3), 26–43.

Hendriksen, S. I., Yang, L., Love, B., & Hall, M. C. (2005). Assessing academic support: The effects of tutoring on student learning outcomes. *Journal of College Reading and Learning, 35*(2), 56–65.

Herve, P. Y., Zago, L., Petit, L., Mazoyer, B., & Tzourio-Mazoyer, N. (2013). Revisiting human hemispheric specialization with neuroimaging. *Trends in Cognitive Sciences, 17*, 69–80.

Huang, G., Taddese, N., & Walter, E. (2000). Entry and persistence of women and minorities in college science and engineering education (No. NCES 2000601). Washington, DC: National Center for Education Statistics.

Hudson, W. (2006). Can an early alert excessive absenteeism warning system be effective in retaining freshman students? *Journal of College Student Retention, 7*(3–4), 217–226.

Hultgren, D. (1970). The role of the individual learning center in effecting educational change. In G. B. Schick & M. M. May (Eds.), *Reading: Process and pedagogy.* National Reading Conference 19th Yearbook 2, 89–94. Milwaukee, WI.

International Tutor Training Program Certification (ITTPC). (2018). Retrieved from https://www.crla.net/index.php/certifications/ittpc-international-tutor-training -program

Jackson, R., & Grutsch McKinney, J. (2017). Beyond tutoring: Mapping the invisible landscape of writing center work. *Praxis: A Writing Center Journal, 9*(1). https://repos itories.lib.utexas.edu/bitstream/handle/2152/62108/Jackson_McKinney%209.1Rais ingtheInstitutionalProfileofWritingCenterWork-10.pdf?sequence=2&isAllowed=y

Jamieson, P. (2003). Designing more effective on-campus teaching and learning spaces: A role for academic developers. *International Journal for Academic Development, 8*(1–2), 119–133. doi:10.1080/1360144042000277991

Janiszewski, C., Noel, H., & Sawyer, A. G. (2003). A meta-analysis of the spacing effect in verbal learning: Implications for research on advertising repetition and consumer memory. *Journal of Consumer Research, 30*, 138–140.

Jarrett, C. J., & Harris, J. A. (2009). SI plus: A program description and an analysis of student feedback. *Learning Assistance Review, 14*(2), 33–42.

Jones, M., & Kolko, V. (2005). The psychosocial growth of peer mentors in a college program for students on academic probation. *Psychosocial Growth of Peer Mentors in College.*

Keenan, C. (2014). *Mapping Student-Lead Peer Learning in the UK.* Higher Education Academy. Retrieved from https://www.heacademy.ac.uk/system/files/re-sources/peer_led_learning_keenan_nov_14-final.pdf

Knight, J. K., & Wood, W. B. (2005). Teaching more by lecturing less. *Cell Biology Education, 4*(4), 298–310.

Kochenour, E. O., Jolley, D. S., Kaup, J. G., Patrick, D. L., Roach, K. D., & Wenzler, L. A. (1997). Supplemental instruction: An effective component of student affairs programming. *Journal of College Student Development, 38*(6), 577–586.

Kostecki, J., & Bers, T. (2008). The effect of tutoring on student success. *Journal of Applied Research in the Community College, 16*(1), 6–12.

Kramer, G. L. (2003). *Student academic services: An integrated approach.* San Francisco, CA: Jossey-Bass.

Krug, D., Davis, B., & Glover, J. A. (1990). Massed versus distributed repeated reading: A case of forgetting helping recall? *Journal of Educational Psychology, 82*, 366–371.

Kuh, G. D. (2015). *Using evidence of student learning to improve higher education.* San Francisco, CA: Jossey-Bass.

Kuh, G., Kinzie, J., Schuh, J., & Whitt, E. (2005). *Student success in college: Creating conditions that matter.* San Francisco, CA: Jossey-Bass.

Kuh, G. D., Schneider, C. G., & Association of American Colleges and Universities. (2008). *High-impact educational practices: What they are, who has access to them, and why they matter.* Washington, DC: Association of American Colleges and Universities.

Laufgraben, J. L., & Shapiro, N. S. (2004). *Sustaining and improving learning communities.* San Francisco, CA: Jossey-Bass.

Lenning, O. T., & Ebbers, L. H. (1999). The powerful potential of learning communities: Improving education for the future. *ASHE-ERIC Higher Education Report 26*(6). Washington, DC: George Washington University, Graduate School of Education and Human Development.

Lerner, N. (1999). Process versus product: A case of goals in conflict. *Journal of College Reading and Learning, 29*(2), 216–222. doi:10.1080/10790195.1999.10 850081

Loots, D. A. (2009). Student involvement and retention in higher education: The case for academic peer mentoring programmes for first-years. *Education as Change, 13*(1), 211–235.

Lunsford, A. (1991). Collaboration, control, and the idea of a writing center. *Writing Center Journal, 12*(1), 3–10. Retrieved from http://www.jstor.org/stable/43441887

Martin, D. C. (1980). Learning centers in professional schools. In K. V. Lauridsen (Ed.), *Examining the scope of learning centers* (pp. 69–79). San Francisco, CA: Jossey-Bass.

Martin, D. C., & Hurley, M. (2005). Supplemental instruction. In M. L. Upcraft, J. N. Gardner, & B. O. Barefoot (Eds.), *Challenging & supporting the first-year student: A handbook for improving the first year of college* (pp. 308–319). San Francisco, CA: Jossey-Bass.

Mason, D., & Verdel, E. (2001). Gateway to success for at-risk students in a large-group introductory chemistry class. *Journal of Chemical Education, 78*(2), 252–255.

McClellan, G. S., Creager, K., & Savoca, M. (2018). *A good job: Campus employment as a high-impact practice.* Sterling, VA: Stylus.

McConnell, P. J. (2000). What community colleges should do to assist first-generation students. *Community College Review, 28*(3), 75–87.

McDaniel, M. A., & Masson, M. E. J. (1985). Altering memory representations through retrieval. *Journal of Experimental Psychology: Learning, Memory, and Cognition, 11*, 371–385.

McKinley, J. (2011). Group workshops: Saving our writing centre in Japan. *Studies in Self-Access Learning Journal, 2*(4), 292–303.

Mesa, D. (2005). *Student-centered operations: A guide to building, implementing, and improving one-stop shops.* Horsham, PA: LRP Publications.

Metz Bemer, A. (2010). *The rhetoric of space in the design of academic computer writing locations* (Unpublished doctoral dissertation). Utah State University, Logan, UT.

Miller, R. L., & Santana-Vega, E. (2006). Can good questions and peer discussion improve calculus instruction? *Primus, 16*(3), 193–203.

Mullin, J., Schorn, S., Turner, T., Hertz, R., Davidson, D., & Baca, A. (2008). Challenging our practices, supporting our theories: Writing mentors as change agents across discourse communities. *Across the Disciplines: A Journal of Language, Learning, and Academic Writing, 5*, 1–10.

Munley, V. G., Garvey, E., & McConnell, M. J. (2010). The effectiveness of peer tutoring on student achievement at the university level. *American Economic Review, 100*(2), 277–282.

National Census of Writing. (2017). Four-year institution survey. Retrieved from http://writingcensus.swarthmore.edu/survey/4

Nealon. J. (2007). One-stop student service centers: Virtual and actual. In N. Sinsabaugh (Ed.), *Student centered financial services: Innovations that succeed* (pp. 1–12). Washington, DC: National Association of College and University Business Officers.

Nielsen, J. A., Zielinski, B. A., Ferguson, M. A., Lainhart, J. E., & Anderson, J. S. An evaluation of the left-brain vs. right-brain hypothesis with resting state functional connectivity magnetic resonance imaging. *PLoS ONE* 8, e71275–11. doi:10.1371/journal.pone.0071275

Ning, H. K., & Downing, K. (2010). The impact of supplemental instruction on learning competence and academic performance. *Studies in Higher Education, 35*(8), 921–939.

North, S. (1984). The idea of a writing center. *College English, 46*(5), 433–446. doi:10.2307/377047

Olaussen, A., Reddy, P., Irvine, S., & Williams, B. (2016). Peer-assisted learning: Time for nomenclature clarification. *Medical Education Online, 21*(1). doi:10.3402/meo.v21.30974

Organisation for Economic Co-operation and Development. (2002). Understanding the brain: Towards a new learning science. Paris: OECD Publishing.

Osman, G. (2007). *Student perceptions of the effectiveness of a mandatory remedial tutorial program in a developmental program at a historically black university* (Unpublished doctoral dissertation). Montgomery, AL: Alabama State University.

Pashler, H., McDaniel, M., Rohrer, D., & Bjork, R. (2008). Learning styles: Concepts and evidence. *Psychological Science in the Public Interest, 9*(3), 103–119.

Peterson, G. T. (1975). *The learning center: A sphere for nontraditional education.* Hamden, CT: Shoestring.

Pew Research Center. (2019a). Internet & technology: Social media fact sheet. Retrieved from https://www.pewresearch.org/internet/fact-sheet/social-media/

Pew Research Center. (2019b). Share of U.S. adults using social media, including Facebook, is mostly unchanged since 2018. Retrieved from https://www.pewre search.org/fact-tank/2019/04/10/share-of-u-s-adults-using-social-media-including -facebook-is-mostly-unchanged-since-2018/

Pfleging, E. (2002). *An evaluation of the early alert program at Columbia College.* Stanislaus, CA: Master of Arts Action Research Project. Retrieved from ERIC database (ED478596)

Price, J., Lumpkin, A. G., Seemann, E. A., & Bell, D. C. (2012). Evaluating the impact of supplemental instruction on short- and long-term retention of course content. *Journal of College Reading and Learning, 42*(2), 8–26.

Puzio, K., & Colby, G. T. (2013). Cooperative learning and literacy: A meta-analytic review. *Journal of Research on Educational Effectiveness, 6*(4), 339–60.

Reinheimer, D., Grace-Odeleye, B., Francois, G., & Kusorgbor, C. (2010). Tutoring: A support strategy for at-risk students. *Learning Assistance Review, 15*(1), 23–33.

Rendleman, E. (2013). Writing centers and mandatory visits, WPA-CompPile research bibliographies, no. 22. WPA-CompPile Research Bibliographies. http://comppile.org/wpa/bibliographies/Bib22/Rendleman.pdf

Rheinheimer, D. C., & McKenzie, K. (2011). The impact of tutoring on the academic success of undeclared students. *Journal of College Reading and Learning, 41*(2), 22–36.

Richland, L. E., Bjork, R. A., Finley, J. R., & Linn, M. C. (2005). Linking cognitive science to education: Generation and interleaving effects. In B. G. Bara, L. Barsalou, & M. Bucciarelli (Eds.), *Proceedings of the twenty-seventh annual conference of the Cognitive Science Society* (pp. 1850–1855). Mahwah, NJ: Lawrence Erlbaum.

Rodby, J. (2002). The subject is literacy: General education and the dialectics of power and resistance in the writing center. In P. Gillespie, A. Gillam, L. F. Brown, & B. Stay (Eds.), *Writing center research: Extending the conversation* (pp. 221–234). Mahwah, NJ: Lawrence Erlbaum.

Rohrer, D. (2012). Interleaving helps students distinguish among similar concepts. *Educational Psychology Review, 24,* 355–367.

Rohrer, D., Dedrick, R. F., & Stershic, S. (2015). Interleaved practice improves mathematics learning. *Journal of Educational Psychology, 107*(3), 900–908.

Rose, D., & Meyer, A. (2002). *Teaching every student in the digital age: Universal design for learning.* Alexandria, VA: Association for Supervision and Curriculum Development.

Sanford, D. (2015). The Peer-Interactive Writing Center at the University of New Mexico. In M. J. Reiff, A. Bawarshi, M. Baliff, & C. Weisser (Eds.), *Ecologies of writing programs: Pprofiles of writing programs in context.* Anderson, SC: Parlor Press.

Sanford, D. (2020). *The Rowman & Littlefield guide for peer tutors.* Lanham, MD: Rowman & Littlefield.

Schader, B. (2007). *Learning commons: Evolution and collaborative essentials.* The Netherlands: Chandos.

Schleyer, G. K., Langdon, G. S., & James, S. (2005). Peer tutoring in conceptual design. *European Journal of Engineering Education, 30*(2), 245–254.

Schmidt, N., & Kaufman, J. (2007). Learning commons: Bridging the academic and student affairs divide to enhance learning across campus. *Research Strategies, 20*, 242–256.

Schmitz, C. S., & Andreozzi, J. (1990). *The first year at General College: Report on year-long interview study of 34 General College freshman (Tech. Rep. No. 3).* Minneapolis, MN: Office of Research and Evaluation, General College, University of Minnesota.

Schroeder, C. (2011). *Coming in from the margins: Faculty development's emerging organizational development role in institutional change.* Sterling, VA: Stylus.

Schulman, L. S. (2005). Signature pedagogies in the professions. *Daedalus, 134*(3), 52–59.

Shamoon, L., & Burns, D. (1995). A critique of pure tutoring. *Writing Center Journal, 15*(2), 134–151.

Shapiro, D., Dundar, A., Huie, F., Wakhungu, P., Yuan, X., Nathan, A., & Hwang, Y. A. (2017). *A national view of student attainment rates by race and ethnicity—fall 2010 cohort (Signature Report No. 12b).* Herndon, VA: National Student Clearinghouse Research Center.

Shapiro, N. S., & Levine, J. J. (1999). *Creating learning communities: A practical guide to winning support, organizing for change, and implementing programs.* San Francisco, CA: Jossey-Bass.

Simons, J. M. (2011). *A national study of student early alert models at four-year institutions of higher education.* Jonesboro, AR: Doctoral dissertation. Retrieved from ProQuest database (UMI 3482551)

Sinclair, Bryan. (2007). Commons 2.0: Library spaces designed for collaborative learning. *EDUCAUSE Quarterly, 30*(4), 1ff.

Slavin, R. E. (1992). When and why does cooperative learning increase achievement? Theoretical and empirical perspectives. In R. Hertz-Lazarowitz & N. Miller (Eds.), *Interaction in cooperative groups: The theoretical anatomy of group learning* (pp. 145–173). New York, NY: Cambridge University Press.

Smith, B. L., MacGregor, J., Matthews, R. S., & Gabelnick, F. (2004). *Learning communities: Reforming undergraduate education.* San Francisco, CA: Jossey-Bass.

Smith, J., Walter, T., & Hoey, G. (1992). Support programs and student self-efficacy: Do first-year students know when they need help? *Journal of the First-Year Experience & Students in Transition, 2*, 41–67.

Smith, K. (2001). Question #17: What are some space, furnishings, and equipment considerations in the design of the LAC?: A conversation with Karen Smith. In F. Christ, R. Sheets, & K. Smith (Eds), *Starting a learning assistance center.* Clearwater, FL: H & H.

Smith, M. A., Blunt, J. R., Whiffen, J. W., & Karpicke, J. D. (2016). Does providing prompts during retrieval practice improve learning? *Applied Cognitive Psychology, 30*, 544–553.

Smith, M. K., Wood, W. B., Adams, W. K., Wieman, C., Knight, J. K., Guild, N., & Su, T. T. (2009). Why peer discussion improves student performance on in-class concept questions. *Science, 323*(5910), 122–124.

Soven, M. (2001). Curriculum-based peer tutors and WAC. In S. H. McLeod, E. Miraglia, M. Soven, & C. Thaiss (Eds.), *WAC for the new millennium: Strategies for continuing writing-across-the-curriculum programs* (pp. 200–232). Urbana, IL: National Council of Teachers of English.

Spaniol-Mathews, P., Letourneau, L. E., & Rice, E. (2016). The impact of online supplemental instruction on academic performance and persistence in undergraduate STEM courses. *Supplemental Instruction Journal, 2*(1), 19–32.

Spenner, K., Buchmann, C., & Landerman, L. R. (2004). The black-white achievement gap in the first college year: Evidence from a new longitudinal case study. *Research in Social Stratification and Mobility, 22*, 187–216.

Spigelman, C., & Grobman, L. (2005). *On location: Theory and practice in classroom-based writing tutoring.* Logan, UT: All USU Press Publications.

Springer, L., Stanne, M. E., & Donovan, S. S. (1999). Effects of small-group learning on undergraduates in science, mathematics, engineering, and technology. *Review of Educational Research, 69*, 21–51.

Stebleton, M. J., & Soria, K. M. (2012). Breaking down barriers: Academic obstacles of first-generation students at research universities. *Learning Assistance Review, 17*(2), 7–19.

Story, M. F., Mace, R. L., & Mueller, J. (1998). *The universal design file: Designing for people of all ages and abilities.* Raleigh, NC: NC State University, Center for Universal Design.

Strayhorn, T. L. (2006). Factors influencing the academic achievement of first-generation college students. *NASPA Journal, 43*(4), 82–111. doi:10.2202/1949-6605.1724

Strauss, V. (2013). Howard Gardner: "Multiple intelligences" are not "learning styles." The Answer Sheet. *Washington Post.* Retrieved from http://www.washington post.com/blogs/answer-sheet/wp/2013/10/16/howard-gardnermultiple-intelli gences-are-not-learning-styles/?tid=auto_complete

Suhr-Sytsma, M., & Brown, S. (2011). Theory in/to practice: Addressing the Everyday language of oppression in the writing center. *Writing Center Journal, 31*(2), 13–49.

Suskie, L. A. (2009). *Assessing student learning: A common sense guide,* 2nd ed. San Francisco, CA: Jossey-Bass.

Tampke, D. R. (2013). Developing, implementing, and assessing an early alert system. *Journal of College Student Retention, 14*(4), 523–532.

Ticknor, C. S., Shaw, K. A., & Howard, T. (2014). Assessing the impact of tutorial services. *Journal of College Reading and Learning, 45*(1), 52–66. doi:10.1080/10 790195.2014.949552

Tillerson, C. W. (1973). *Effects of a learning center method versus lecture method of teaching as related to achievement, self-concept, and attitude of college fresh-*

men (Doctoral dissertation). Available from ProQuest Dissertations and Theses database (UMI No. 7312930)

Tinto, V., Russo, P., & Kadel, S. (1994). Constructing educational communities: Increasing retention in challenging circumstances. *AACC Journal* (February/March), 26–29.

Toms, M., & Reedy, D. (2016). National College Learning Center Association 2014 survey report. *Learning Assistance Review, 21*(1), 9–18.

Topping, K. J. (1996). The effectiveness of peer tutoring in further and higher education: A typology and review of the literature. *Higher Education, 32*, 321–345.

Topping, K. J., & Ehly, S. W. (2001). Peer assisted learning: A framework for consultation. *Journal of Educational and Psychological Consultation, 12*(2), 113–132. doi:10.1207/S1532768XJEPC1202_03

Trammell, J., & Bruce, J. (2008). Utilizing multiple interlocking learning communities to form a center for teaching and learning. *Learning Assistance Review, 13*(1), 47–57.

Trowbridge, S., Waterbury, C., & Sudbury, L. (2017). Learning in bursts: Microlearning with social media. Educause Review. Retrieved from https://er.educause.edu/articles/2017/4/learning-in-bursts-microlearning-with-social-media

Truman, J. (2019). On brand: Communication center tutors as social media content creators. *Communication Center Journal, 5*(1), 134–144.

Truschel, J., & Reedy, D. (2009). National survey—What is a learning center in the 21st century? *Learning Assistance Review, 14*(1), 9–22.

Tzourio-Mazoyer, N., Crivello, F., & Mazoyer, B. (2017). Is the planum temporale surface area a marker of hemispheric or regional language lateralization? *Brain Structure and Function.* doi:10.1007/s00429-017-1551-7

Valles, S. B., Babcock, R. D., & Jackson, K. K. (2017). Writing center administrators and diversity: A survey. *Peer Review, 1*(1). thepeerreview-iwca.org/issues/issue-1/writing-center-administrators-and-diversity-a-survey

Velasco, J. B., & Stains, M. (2015). Exploring the relationships between perceptions of tutoring and tutoring behaviours: A focus on graduate students serving as peer tutors to college-level chemistry students. *Chemistry Education Research and Practice, 16*, 856–868. doi:10.1039/C5RP00103J

Wagner, T. D., Phan, L. K., Liberzon, I., & Taylor, S. F. (2003). Valence, gender, and lateralization of functional brain anatomy in emotion: a meta-analysis of findings from neuroimaging. *NeuroImage, 19*, 513–531.

Walker, C., McHargue, M., McClure, R., & Adams, N. (1974). A learning assistance center at Stanford? In G. Kerstiens (Ed.), *Reading update: Ideals to reality. Proceedings of the seventh annual conference of the Western College Reading Association* (pp. 183–188). Oakland, CA: WCRA.

Whitman, N. A. (1988). Types of peer teaching used in higher education. *ASHE-ERIC Higher Education Report, 17*, 13–32. doi:10.1002/aehe.3640170405

Whitt, E. J., Schuh, J. H., Kinzie, J., & Kuh, G. D. (2013). *Student success in college: Creating conditions that matter.* San Francisco, CA: Jossey-Bass.

Xu, Y., Hartman, S., Uribe, G., & Mencke, R. (2014). The effects of peer tutoring on undergraduate students' final examination scores in mathematics. *Journal of College Reading and Learning, 32*, 22–31.

Yockey, F. A., & George, A. A. (2000). The effects of a freshman seminar paired with supplemental instruction. *Journal of the First-Year Experience and Students in Transition, 10*(2), 57–76.

Zacharopoulou, A., Giles, M., & Condell, J. (2015). Enhancing PASS leaders' employability skills through reflection. *Journal of Learning Development in Higher Education.* Special Edition: Academic Peer Learning. Retrieved from https://journal.aldinhe.ac.uk/index.php/jldhe/article/view/348/pdf

Zha, S., Estes, M. D., & Xu, L. (2019). A meta-analysis on the effect of duration, task, and training in peer-led learning. *Journal of Peer Learning, 12*, 5–28.

Index

About the Authors

Daniel R. Sanford, PhD, is director of the Center for Teaching and Learning at Boise State University. Before that he was director of writing and the Academic Resource Commons at Bates College and director of the Center for Academic Program Support at the University of New Mexico. He is an experienced learning center administrator and a recognized scholar and professional in the field of peer tutoring. He is also a cognitive scientist, the author of numerous articles in the field of cognitive linguistics, and an experienced educator with a wealth of experience making the mechanisms of the brain accessible and intuitive to college-age students.

Michelle Steiner, PhD, is assistant vice president for student success at Marymount University. An experienced professional in the fields of academic advising and learning center administration, she has previously directed undergraduate academic advising in the Columbian College of Arts & Sciences at George Washington University and peer tutoring for the Center for Academic Program Support (CAPS) at the University of New Mexico. Under her directorship, the National College Learning Center Association awarded CAPS the annual Frank L. Christ Outstanding Learning Center Award in 2012 for the best undergraduate learning center at a four-year college. Dr. Steiner is a psychologist and an active scholar in the field of learning center administration.